The Blind Palmist

LAWRENCE TYLER

✧ ✧ ✧ ✧ ✧ ✧

The Blind Palmist

*Being an Often Humorous Account
of an American Teacher's
Year in China*

Harbinger House
TUCSON · NEW YORK

HARBINGER HOUSE, INC.
Tucson, Arizona

© 1990 Lawrence Tyler
Photography © 1990 Lawrence Tyler, Tina Lee
All rights reserved
Manufactured in the United States of America
∞ This book was printed on acid-free, archival quality paper
Typeset in 10½ point Linotron 202 Galliard
Designed by Kaelin Chappell

Library of Congress Cataloging-in-Publication Data
Tyler, Lawrence, 1940-
    The blind palmist : being an often humorous account of
an American teacher's year in China / Lawrence Tyler.
       p.   cm.
    ISBN 0-943173-53-1 (alk. paper)
    1. China—Social life and customs—1976-   I. Title.
DS779.23.T95   1990   90-33030
951.05 ' 8—dc20

CONTENTS

Preface   vii

Introduction   I

ONE   Getting There   4
Leaving / Hong Kong / Guangzhou Airport /
Guilin / Chinese Trains / Nanning

TWO   Teaching: Paradoxes and Symbols   14
Break of Day / Class Time / Exam Time /
Censoring / Tongue Mobilization / Tough Nuts /
The Party / Mantras / The Library / Group
Photographs

THREE   Pains of Socialism, Joys of Socializing   36
Health / Banquets / Art and Entertainment /
Mail / Free Conversation / Friendship Stores /
Foreign Aid / The Fork vs. Chopsticks

FOUR   Street Scenes   53
Dying Guys Don't Beg / Roadside / Sleep / Beasts
of the Fields / Red Eyes / Fashion / Great
Expectorations / A Rube Goldberg Solution /
Television / Running Amok / Changing Money

FIVE   Excursions   75
To Rongxian / To Dali and Beyond / Raiders of the
Lost Flashlight

SIX   Pride and Prejudice   93
        *The Blind Palmist / Coming to Terms / The Ethic
        of Mediocrity / Hospitality / The Emperor's
        Household / Theocracy / China or "Not" / Relative
        Freedoms / The Myth of Modernization*

SEVEN   Leaving   112
        *Going Home / Amusing the Stone / Remembering
        There*

        Appendix
        Thirty-Three Things to Do or Think about to Make   117
        *a Year in China Less Uncomfortable (In No
        Particular Order)*

        Ten Chinese Bureaucratic Rules of the Game   123
        When Dealing with Foreigners

PREFACE

As I prepared this manuscript for publication, the events of the May-June 1989 student rebellion in Beijing unfolded. Thousands of students converged on Tiananmen Square to demonstrate for democracy and freedom of expression. In the aftermath of the bloody denial of that quest, the units of the 27th Field Army and the 28th Field Army confronted one another in and around Beijing. Among the Communist party leadership purges seemed imminent. The student leadership was facing criminal charges and the swift, certain penalties of Chinese justice. All the familiar initial stages of civil war again threatened to spread chaos throughout the country.

From coverage by U.S. television (unavailable to me in Malaysia), it must have appeared as though the entire society and culture of China were changing direction in a matter of weeks. Certainly, the lives of the young participants—soldiers and students—were unalterably changed. The worst consequence is that, as during the Cultural Revolution of the late 1960s, the aspirations of another generation have been quashed. Silencing China's best minds has become a tragic, crippling pattern.

It is important to recognize that these events were better reported and scrutinized around the world than within China. The demonstrations, so dramatic in their unfolding and tragic in culmination, seemed to reveal to the world a student body united for change and an army divided in loyalty. Yet what was also revealed, perhaps less obviously to TV viewers, was how large a stone must be thrown into the vast sea of China in order for the ripples to reach a shoreline. The violent confrontation of thousands in the capital caused few perceptible tremors in China's distant regions. In the end, as these events revealed the desperate desire for reform, they also revealed the nepotism and warlord mentality of China's real power structure. I say, "in the end"; but the Chinese know that for such dynamics there is no end—only an endless unfolding.

The politics and ideology of the Communist party were obviously the constraining context of living in China, but always of more interest to me were the means by which ordinary Chinese people, and the foreigners who lived among them, negotiated their days, bringing as much stability and civility as possible into their lives. To honor that, I have left my observations essentially as I wrote them at the time.

LAWRENCE TYLER
Petaling Jaya, Malaysia

The Blind Palmist

One of Dali's pagodas

INTRODUCTION

Many travelers blame their wanderlust on childhood exposure to the pages of *National Geographic,* but not me. That publication was and is too graphic to stimulate my fantasies. Maps, however, have always gotten me into trouble: their contours are suggestive, even vaguely lurid in the manner they invite detailed inspection. I have been aroused far more often by Rand McNally's foldouts than by Hugh Hefner's centerfolds.

I share this vice with the composer Frederick Delius, who, while browsing through an atlas, became fixated on the languidly dangling shape of Florida. He badgered his father into investing in a citrus plantation, booked passage, and for the next year watched oranges fall to the ground as he became obsessed with musical study. Maps do that. They attract you to a place for all the wrong reasons. The fortunate traveler, however, finds unanticipated reasons for staying.

Like all travel literature, this book is about places seen and people met—in this case, when my wife, Mary, and I lived and taught in southern China. That sounds straightforward enough, as though I were writing about an event with a clear beginning and an end.

A beginning can be located. In my journal, I noted the day and hour when I was asked if I wanted to take a position in China for one year. I can recall telling Mary that the offer had come and that we had to decide if we were serious about a change of direction in the middle of our lives. We were in the kitchen of our house (which I have missed nearly every day since).

Immediately, I was filled with that mixture of dread and elation travelers experience when they contemplate leaving a beloved home.

Soon after arriving in China, the first wave of letters from home invariably asked, "Do you like it there?" A logical, sensible question. Yet, it was bafflingly difficult to answer. Yes or no just didn't seem to approach the matter. I tried to think of comparisons or similes to convey the situation. Most of the time I answered with a variation on one of the following:

1. China is not to be liked or disliked: it is simply to be absorbed by your senses. It's like being in a car crash while your radio is playing Mozart. A part of you is entranced while another part is being jarred to hell.

2. Being in China is like climbing a mountain you don't know is there: you keep thinking it should get easier with experience, but every step takes you into thinner air.

Neither of these aphorisms could really communicate any sense of the China experience to friends at home.

I wish I could portray myself as one of those travelers in search of enlightenment or altered consciousness. The reader of these pages will soon find I am not so spiritually motivated. All I have ever wanted is to understand my world, and for me that world always comes down to the people I encounter and the setting in which we meet. My understanding is based in listening very closely to what people say, watching very closely as they say it, and paying attention to where I am.

During my time in China, however, I caught glimpses of other ways of knowing—including that of the blind palmist. She sat Buddhalike, unsighted but all-knowing, telling fortunes in hands she could not see, while surrounded by the trappings of Marxist Realism. Whether or not her customers believed her, they clearly found more comfort in her version of their future than in that of their local party secretary. By luck or destiny, she came along just when I most needed her. Even if I couldn't share her vision, she inadvertently gave me another way of seeing China.

As I said, I can point to a beginning of the China journey; the ending is less clear. By serendipity (or for the stone's amusement), I am now residing in Malaysia and have lived three of the last four years in Asia. In a sense, being in Malaysia is a part of having been in China. So, I can't yet isolate an ending as I can a beginning.

My China year was nearly four years ago, but like any meaningful travel, it is still ongoing.

ONE

✧ ✧ ✧ ✧ ✧ ✧ ✧

Getting There

Leaving

On our flight from San Francisco, the in-flight movie was *A Room with a View*. The entire front row was occupied by a group of young blind men and their guide dogs. The blind men all leaned forward, engrossed in their conversation, wonderfully oblivious to the enlarged images of Margaret Smith and the other actors. The film flickered eighteen inches away; but, as they were not equipped with headsets for the soundtrack, for them the film wasn't there. Throughout my months in China, my language limitations were to make me equally oblivious to the events of my surroundings.

It wasn't the absence of sound in my case, but rather the absence of a complete language comprehension that turns sound into communication (though, I must say, my wife and I studied Mandarin from tapes before we left, and took lessons twice a week while there). Most of the time this was regrettable, but it was a blessing in disguise when trying to sleep in a Chinese faculty tenement. At all hours of the day and night, someone was awake and conversing in our building. My deficiency turned language into background noise that could be slept through. I never did learn whether insomnia was widespread in China or if there were just too many bodies per apartment to sleep all at once; but at 3:00 A.M., my ignorance was bliss.

Hong Kong

Our night flight from Tokyo raced a typhoon to Hong Kong and beat it by hours. Heavy rains were beginning as we checked into our hotel. Hong Kong hotels, along with those of Singapore and Bangkok, set the quality standard for modern Asia. Like everything in Asia, they are labor-intensive (or by American standards overstaffed). Anyone who goes on to a prolonged stay in China and has any experience beyond the few luxury hotels there (such as the White Swan in Guangzhou and the Jianguo in Beijing) soon grows wistful over the service and comfort available in Hong Kong. For most China travelers, it is the last dose of material indulgence before experiencing socialist reality.

Poverty is clearly evident, even by Asian standards. The side-by-side presence of high tech and squalor makes Hong Kong a better preview of the future than Epcot Center. From our hotel-room window, I could look across the narrow street to open windows where men and women stooped over treadle sewing machines all day. The single-room apartments in the same buildings were a strong reminder that material poverty is the norm for most people in the world. But in Hong Kong, the poverty does not seem as inescapable as it does in India, Nepal, or the areas of Asia where the poor are trapped in a religion and tradition that reinforces the status quo. The attitude of laborers here seems to be that though they aren't rich yet, they're working at it. The hotel servers do things with civility, not servility. Even the self-described "room boy" who woke us from a jet-lag coma (to inquire if he could turn the bedcovers down and leave Godiva chocolates on the pillow) was more amused than chagrined at disturbing us. I took the chocolates and stumbled back to bed.

The next morning at breakfast we watched two "inspectors" inspect the dining room as ostentatiously as Clouseau searching for a clue or covering his bungling. It required two of them because the male needed a female assistant to carry his clipboard. He stared at the ceiling, stomped the floor, shook the rails, rubbed the tables, and so on, while the woman responded to his orders with check marks on the list. Everything was checked twice, in case something had deteriorated behind their backs. They managed to make a morning of it.

This remains fixed in my mind partly because of the display they made of their work and partly because once we were in China we would never again see any sign of maintenance inside any public building. On the campus where we lived in the coming months, one of the first sounds each morning was the scratching of brooms on the pavement and hard-packed earth: female sweepers, with brooms made from branches and dried bushes, were starting their daily sweeping of the entire campus. Yet the apartment we were moved into had not been cleaned since it was last inhabited, two years previously. The classrooms were cursorily cleaned twice a year by the students. New buildings became occupied before the rubble of construction was cleaned from the floors. Never in a year of living and traveling did I see a public toilet that appeared or smelled as though it had ever been cleaned, but the streets always got swept.

Guangzhou Airport

China's national airline, CAAC, is a good introduction to the country. Much as particles randomly exchange and recombine in subatomic physics, so do CAAC's planes exist. Before a traveler's glazed and wondering eyes, flights are scheduled, rescheduled, canceled, or simply forgotten. They neither arrive nor depart, yet continually exist in theory and in schedule. Like the mythical Flying Dutchman, they are out there somewhere, nearing but never achieving their destination—a moral lesson to those who would leave home.

Guangzhou's airport and Customs are a classic example of the labor-intensive employment that characterizes China's public works and facilities. Beginning at the airport runway, very young military personnel and civilian employees are stationed at arm's length from one another. Each has a tiny, well-guarded task to facilitate or impede the process, depending on your own role in this gauntlet. Eventually we snake-danced through Immigration and Customs and arrived at the traveler's abyss of "What happens next?". There were no signs or clues in any language.

Always in China as you arrive at the edge, however, a stranger emerges to save you. This is the Chinese version of Traveler's Aid. It happened to us in Guangzhou, and it would happen again—in Guilin, Kunming, Beijing, and Chengdu. Other foreigners in China told us of the same experience. From this, the astute "foreign guest" can observe at least two points:

1. Many Chinese want to be helpful to foreigners. In doing so, they will usually profess the importance of friendship between countries and people. More practically, helping foreigners accords them the rare opportunity to practice their foreign language (usually English) and to interact with a foreigner in a situation not planned and overseen by the government. There is even the remote possibility that such a chance encounter could flourish into long-term contact with a foreigner. Most educated Chinese want to make such contacts. Everywhere in the world, people who live with limited possibilities acquire the habit of playing long shots. In

Michigan, such people buy lottery tickets; in China, many make a habit of helping foreigners.

This may sound like a very cynical view of help freely given, but all I am suggesting is that foreigners are aided and valued in China for several reasons. One may be genuine and uncomplicated friendliness. But at another level, a foreigner always represents opportunity to those whose own opportunities are very limited. Just remember, in China things are always just what they appear to be and a great deal other than they appear to be.

2. You as a foreigner are never unobserved in China. I do not mean to suggest anything sinister; I merely mean you will never blend in or disappear in the crowd. You are always the focus of attention. Sometimes this is perfectly clear, as when groups of Chinese stop to observe what you are buying or eating or discussing. Your most mundane actions and your everyday appearance will at times mesmerize clusters of children and adults. Other times, in streets and shops, you will think you are going unnoticed. Don't kid yourself. You still stand out like a jeweled elephant and all of those apparently unaware bystanders are waiting to see if you are going to perform tricks or run berserk.

Meanwhile, back at the Guangzhou airport, a young woman of great charm, intelligence, and fluent English (obviously barred by her competence from participation in the snake dance) took us in hand and led us across the airport to the one CAAC ticket counter, where a handful of ticket agents were mangling tickets, luggage tags, and passports. As chimps could ultimately write Shakespeare on a typewriter, so possibly could these fellows eventually have processed a ticket. They looked at our ticket coupons for Guilin, deeply suspicious and somehow intuiting that a single U.S. travel agent at her console had stolen the employment of at least forty of their occupational brethren. Our female savior literally took the ticket packets from this sea of thumbs, extracted the proper coupons, and applied the necessary tags and labels to our bags. We extracted ourselves from the sporting crowd that had gathered to watch.

At the end of another gauntlet of teenage soldiers with stamps and punches was a huge waiting room, full even by Asian standards. It was the size of a football field, with the noise level and good-time atmosphere of kickoff time. In one corner, a black-and-white TV screen was filled with the blurred image of a leopard sleeping or some equally exciting scene from a Chinese nature program. From speakers hung high on the arched ceiling, literally above the crowd noise, there emerged the muddy sounds of "The Battle Hymn of the Republic." The Chinese love massive choral groups, and this recording could have been the Mormon Tabernacle Choir or the choir of the People's Liberation Army. Once in a while, almost like a subliminal message under the crowd noise and the choir, a plane departure announcement could be heard. Taking no chances, we found some people with the same numbers on their boarding passes and watched them as closely as kung fu opponents, mirroring their every move until our feints and postures led us to the plane for Guilin.

Guilin

In Guilin we were met at the airport by Zhi Xian (our university liaison) of the foreign languages department of Guangxi University, where we were to teach. The 10 P.M. flight arrived relatively on time, and in a display of rushing, which I learned was part of impressing foreigners, we were trotted to the baggage area to identify our luggage (and not allowed to carry it ourselves) and then trotted to a waiting car for our first experience of Chinese traffic.

The streets in China are a mass of bicycles, pedestrians, pony carts, occasional trucks, vans, or cars, and the unwieldy three-wheeled tractors used as tandem haulers. The primary law of the road is that the largest moving object has the right-of-way. The sensation of dodging through all this is entirely different in a car than on a bicycle. A car ride in China is a true power trip, because even now relatively few Chinese ever get inside a car (buses are a different matter). The Chinese driver's progress and credibility seem to depend entirely on very short bursts of speed, as he or she accelerates and brakes through little unoccupied spaces cleared by honking. Our driver for those two days in Guilin did a great impersonation of a Stephen King character—a road zombie whose tenuous link to life was via the horn.

In the months ahead, we would view everything from the seat of a bicycle. This is a much more immediate experience. Bicyclists are at times pressed together so closely it seems they are all part of some quantum physics experiment to see if several objects can occupy the same space simultaneously while remaining oblivious to one another. Minor accidents go seemingly unnoticed by those involved. This no-fault approach saves face and is efficacious, as little or no compensation is possible anyway. Bundles of sprouts, strings of meat, or loads of charcoal are sorted out, and the cyclists pedal on their way, hardly exchanging a glance. I once saw a woman prying her handlebars from around the leg of a man on a motorcycle; he was turned the other direction, holding an undisturbed conversation with someone else.

The worst misconceptions foreigners bring with them to China are the visual images from coffee-table books of China's scenic wonders. Most of China looks like what it is: either a run-down neighborhood, a poverty area, or a depleted natural resource. I think that is why the exceptional place of beauty seems so perfect when finally seen. Any place of beauty that has survived 4,000 years of neglect, overuse, and abuse is perfect, indeed.

China does assault all the senses of a first-time visitor, but for me the primary sensory impressions were sound, then smell, then taste, then sight and touch. The first three are constantly being overloaded, as I would learn in the months ahead.

Chinese Trains

With only a couple of days' delay, we were able to get "soft-seat" accommodations on the train to Nanning. There are four classes of train travel in China:

SOFT SLEEPER. This often costs more than an air ticket to the same destination. Very few Chinese travel this way; yet the tickets are scarce because they are held back in case a *cadre* (leader) suddenly wants one. (The same practice applies to air travel: You can spend days getting an air ticket, only to find the plane 10 to 20 percent empty when it takes off.)

HARD SLEEPER. Once you are adjusted to the reality of travel in China, this seems an adequate level of luxury. It is a board bunk to lie down on when traveling overnight.

SOFT SEAT. This is a perfectly comfortable way to travel. Roomy, padded chairs face one another separated by a tiny tea table with the ubiquitous thermos of boiled water. Overhead, a small revolving fan provides air conditioning.

HARD SEAT. Suicide is preferable. It is bench seating, sold to standing-room capacity. Acquaintances with bad judgment have traveled overnight never getting close to the bench. Fortunately, it is too crowded for you to fall down. Train toilets range from disgusting to endurable. The seasoned China traveler takes a dose of Lomotil or some other antidiuretic before starting an overnight trip.

One of the luxuries of soft-seat class is recorded entertainment, piped in over strategically located speakers. Without warning, you suddenly receive a full-bore blast of Chinese Muzak—

which sounds to the unschooled foreign ear like Led Zeppelin playing Vivaldi—at a volume that makes it foreground (not background) music. There are no background sounds in China. All radios, TVs, and recorders are played at full volume, as if to get more use from the machine.

The music is interspersed with what sounds like a Chinese version of Abbott and Costello. The Chinese love what they call "cross-talk" comedy routines. There are several very popular comedy teams who specialize in this sort of performance. Typically, one will be a short, chubby Costello type. These duos exploit the almost unlimited potential for verbal confusion built into a tonal language. The changes of meaning intonation gives to the same sound can create the same hilarity for the Chinese audience that Abbott and Costello's "Who's on first?" did for a generation of Americans. (Of course, we Westerners struggling to speak the language can do the same thing without trying.) For most of the seven-hour ride to Nanning, we soft-seaters were grandly entertained by cross-talk and patriotic songs.

Nanning

At the Nanning train station we were met by Mr. Yeo. My first impression was of the White Rabbit: he rushed and fussed in the "impressing foreigner" manner, which was neither efficient nor appropriate to the blistering, humid August weather. Ultimately, our luggage was placed in the trunk of a Russian-built auto called a Lada. The extra weight made the sides of the car rub against the tires whenever we turned a corner. Socialist cars are for people who own nothing.

Nanning, the capital of Guangxi Province,* is a city of "more than a million people" (demography is more an art than a science in China). Until the late 1950s, Nanning had been a small and not very significant town. But its location at the Chinese end of a rail line to Hanoi suddenly made it an important staging area when China was supporting North Vietnam's military efforts. Nanning continues to be a boomtown, in that the entire city is being subjected to waves of razing and reconstruction. A shop or an entire street will be doing business one day and demolished the next.

The traditional construction design in a southern Chinese city is for the second story of buildings to overhang the sidewalk, which satisfies the need for shade and during monsoon weather offers some protection from the rain. But here, like everywhere else in China, traditional form is being replaced by what I call "socialist heroic concrete": uncompromising vertical slabs soaring as high as the budget will permit.

When we arrived in 1986, there were about thirty Westerners (including Japanese, who seemed Western in this setting) living in Nanning. In addition, the occasional consultant or touring scholar shuttled in and out. At the National Day banquet on October 1, the party leaders were able to raise our contingent to about seventy by bringing in foreigners from as far away as Luizhou, sixty kilometers away.

This should indicate how unprepared the city was to accommodate foreign tastes and habits. Every one of us, as well, initially was ill prepared for life in Nanning. Though we acclimated and accommodated at various rates, there is a natural cycle of attitudes foreigners go through if they remain in China long enough. The initial stage is to forgive, accept, and overlook just about any situation. After all, we want to be good guests.

*The proper name of Guangxi Province is Guangxi Zhuang Autonomous Region. This is an acknowledgment by the Chinese government that its population includes many distinct ethnic groups, of which the Zhuang are the most numerous. Guangxi and Yunnan provinces are a part of China in which groups such as the Zhuang, Yi, Dai, Mia, Bai, Sani, and others still retain a core of their own culture and traditions while acknowledging the political authority of the Chinese government.

TWO

✧ ✧ ✧ ✧ ✧ ✧ ✧

Teaching
Paradoxes and Symbols

Break of Day

A typical teaching day began with my alarm clock declaring 5:50 A.M. I set it for that time because I refused to allow the loudspeaker of the Communist state to be the first thing I heard in the morning. The campus-wide broadcast of recorded Chinese revelry blasted through the morning air at 6:00 A.M. If I had to get up at that hour I would do it myself, not wait another ten minutes for a bunch of Communists to do it to me—a petty bourgeois triumph, but it is by such means that the illusion of personal choice is maintained under authoritarian rule.

The blaring, fuzzy recording began with stirring military airs aimed at inspiring everyone to spring from bed for further struggle in the Revolution. This was followed by a perky-voiced Chinese Jane Fonda leading the count for morning calisthenics. If exercise meant living longer under existing conditions, hardly anyone was tempted. A few fanatics had already started their jogging routines before "Jane" started yelling cadence, and small groups of oldsters did Tai Chi to a different drummer; but most people who were out of their beds had started tea or were off to market to beat the crowd.

The recorded exercise segment was followed by an incredible jumble of more musical perkiness: sometimes Western circus music ("The Brave Bulls" got a lot of play), always something by Stephen Foster, interspersed with Chinese pop music, and almost certainly "The Red River Valley"—a great favorite throughout China. The tale is that this and a lot of Stephen Foster music were introduced to Mao and his fellow Long March survivors by Agnes Smedley, the American journalist who became a great "friend of China," as Western converts to the Revolution are called. If so, Agnes has a lot to answer for.

The music was punctuated with approved announcements of the day's events, and the broadcast continued for at least a half hour to roust out the most determined bed-clinger.

But if you did not depend on the bowls of rice noodle served up at the dining halls for your nourishment, you were already headed for the market with shopping basket in hand. There, in semidarkness, you squatted down next to a pile of cabbage or tray of tofu to play Monte Hall with the produce moguls of the free market. Many of these peasants are Zhuang tribesmen, whose dialect confuses even the Chinese, but money talk is the most easily communicated everywhere in the world. (By the second semester, my own language skill had plateaued and did not increase one iota the rest of the year. I actually began to take a perverse pride in how widely I could travel and transact with the tiniest of vocabulary. In Chinese, I had the communication skills of a dyslexic with glossolalia; yet I could buy cabbage, airline tickets, cough syrup, electrical cords, and brandy and ask directions when I got lost.) At any rate, at the morning market soon you had a lot of roughage and a little protein for the day. This left enough time for an unleisurely breakfast before classes began at 7:30 A.M. I never acquired a taste for *congee* (rice gruel), so we heavily supported the local egg industry, eating as many eggs per day as Chinese families could afford for the week.

Class Time

All my classes were scheduled from 7:30 to 11:30 A.M. My classroom was a fourth-floor cavern designed to accommodate about fifty students. Only first-class foreign hotels and the very newest, most important government buildings have elevators. Given the absence of maintenance and the constant presence of crowds, elevators in China would only be accidents waiting to happen.

The classroom was lighted with bare fluorescent bulbs, but on sunny days it needed no lighting, as there were only two or three randomly placed, shredded window curtains. There was no janitorial staff for the classroom buildings, even though dozens of people swept leaves from the campus streets every day.

In theory, the students were to clean the classroom. They did so at the beginning of each semester, whether it needed doing or not. As they were armed only with rags, their work consisted primarily of rearranging the dust. And, as they had never seen a clean classroom or a mopped floor, they had nothing to judge their work by. Each day students would wipe off their own chairs and tables with scraps of newsprint.

About half the windowpanes were broken. In Nanning's semitropical climate, this made little temperature difference to us—except from January through March when wet, forty-degree winter set in. Then I taught wearing a quilted vest and jacket. The wind blowing through the room rearranged the drifts and dunes of chalk dust that collected in the chalk tray over the semester.

There was nothing bad about these conditions; as far as I could tell, this was a very normal Chinese classroom. Other foreign teachers all over the country adjust to similar conditions. Broken windows seem to be the norm. A colleague up north in Xian taught during the coldest months wearing his overcoat and gloves.

My students, juniors and seniors, were a year or two younger than their Western equivalents. They also seemed younger emotionally, due to their upbringing and limited experiences of the world. At an age when Western students have part- or full-time jobs, cars, separate residences, and personal responsibilities, Chinese students remain wholly dependent on their parents and the state. They are to concentrate on study and nothing else. They don't have part-time jobs. "Student help," commonplace throughout Western universities in offices, kitchens, groundskeeping, and so forth, is not part of the Chinese system. So the students depend on the state for tuition and books and on their families for everything else. They are to study and to sublimate their libidos on the athletic fields.

In the workers' "classless" society, accident of birth remains the major determinant of status, especially in rural areas where schools are poor and ill equipped. Throughout their education, students are tracked; in middle school and high school, they're examined to determine how far and in what direction their education will continue. Whether a university-aged young man or woman is a student or a worker depends on quality of schooling, family sacrifice, academic ability, personal effort, government policy, and (often) bribery. Thus, many laborers, especially construction workers on campus, are the same age as the students, but there is no contact between them. They exist separately, without acknowledging one another. It isn't even snobbery; they are just so separate it never occurs to either that they would speak or interact. There are students and there are workers; you are one or the other.

So, the student subculture is designed to be a self-absorbed one, with all attention focused on itself. The students know their life-style is a financial effort for their family, but it is the burden that every family desires—a child who will become part of the educated elite. The work and duty of the student is to not be distracted from succeeding.

Aside from their hormones and libido, their major distraction is that they are usually hungry. Their diet is limited and low in protein. Each morning in the dining hall they are served congee, perhaps with a steamed bun. Lunch is a bowl of rice or rice noodles, with green vegetables and a little meat. Dinner is more of the same. By late morning, their attention and performance are visibly diminished. I don't mean to imply they are being starved, but they never have to worry about excess calories.

Exam Time

Giving an exam in a Chinese classroom is a cultural experience. It is simply impossible for young Chinese to not discuss the exam. I mean they literally *can't* not talk about it. The idea of a group of Chinese being quiet is, in itself, strange and foreign. Noise, sound, and speech are a natural part of their environment. Their congenial, crowded homes and communally focused education make them uneasy in silence.

The most attentive female students sitting in the front row, for no reason apparent to me, would go from rapt attention to what I can only describe as a "whisper frenzy": For one or two minutes, with their noses almost touching, they would buzz and hiss (as only speakers of Cantonese can), then just as suddenly settle back into full attention. Their expressions seemed to convey, "There! That's out of our systems. What a relief."

Exam talk is more relaxed, like the shoptalk between co-workers. My attempts to institute silence during examinations left me frustrated—and them baffled by my irritation. Trying to rearrange the seating to separate conversationalists proved useless. The conversations just became "long distance," incorporating

Mary and her first-year English students

A gardener in Nanning Park

The fading influence of Chairman Mao

message-bearers and intermediaries. And it complicated the arrangements of shared texts, dictionaries, and paper tablets.

Not only do they share texts (even though they're all furnished copies by the department), they also share eyeglasses. As one student writes his answers, another will take the reading glasses from his head to read the blackboard or book. (Many Chinese students have poor vision, which they remedy by buying reading glasses from street peddlers.) Two or three pairs of glasses will travel up and down a classroom as students seek out the lenses giving them the clearest vision. There's surprisingly little fuss over having glasses stripped from one's head in midsentence. They just give their comrades a moment of clear vision and then take them back.

Do they also share information and answers? Of course. It's not even something they conceal. After all, they enter the university together, take all their classes together for four years, eat all their meals together in the dining hall, live eight persons to a room in their dormitory, and have enforced political study every week in which the Communist ethic is stressed. Their identity, and all their experience from infancy, are group oriented.

That is the nature of Confucian-based Chinese Communism. There is no way for a foreign schoolteacher who is the only outsider in the room to fight it. I was forced to recognize I was teaching Chinese to use English, not teaching Chinese to be Americans.

My own solution (or capitulation) was to give open-book exams—long, involved open-book exams that gave each little huddle of students a workout flipping pages, reading, writing, discussing, and sharing spectacles and answers. I clung to the illusion that it was a good learning experience, and they reinforced my belief by groaning, shaking their heads, sighing, appearing puzzled, seeming to be involved in Herculean efforts, and taking every available second of the exam time before turning in their communally arrived at individual exams.

I also learned to not be offended if their exams were written on wrapping paper or what we would consider trash paper. They used the tiniest and shabbiest scraps of paper because it was costly and not to be wasted.

As an antidote to the deathless poetics of Wordsworth and to ensure that they read something without thee's and thou's, I gave my British literature class an article on "The New Technology." It included a statement to the effect that typewriters and file cabinets were being made obsolete by electronic data-retrieval systems and computers. So I was slowly, meticulously explaining as well as I could about electronic data-retrieval systems and computers when a student hesitantly raised his hand and respectfully asked, "What is a file cabinet?" As it was an act of trust and bravery for a student to ask any question, I carefully did not laugh and just as carefully explained it. Actually, I consider that class period a success, as one student did learn about a new piece of technology—the file cabinet.

Censoring

At about the same time other universities were having student demonstrations for more "democracy," one of the reading assignments in my British literature class was John Milton's *Areopagitica*—not exactly my idea of how to spend a morning, but it was in the state-approved textbook. Therefore I and the class read aloud one of the earliest, most passionate, certainly the most literate of cries for the freedoms of expression and the press to be found in the English language. This had been pretty heady stuff for Puritans and Presbyterians, and I was a bit apprehensive of its effect on young Sino-Communists. But I needn't have worried: it turned out the Chinese censors knew far better than I the calming influence of Milton's style on uncomprehending readers.

During the lesson, my mind began to wander a bit as I fantasized the Chinese censors hacking their way through

Milton's thicket of allusive phrases. I could see their conference tables arranged in the usual square-doughnut formation. They were sitting in proper bureaucratic posture with both feet flat on the floor, knees together, their hands symmetrically poised on the armrests of the high-backed chairs, which, of course, were draped in antimacassars. Each identically seated censor had a standardized covered mug of tepid tea in front of him or her. So convened, they were slowly, tortuously deliberating on whether to include in the state-approved English text Milton's plea for the (literally) unlicensed expression of all ideas. I am sure they arrived at their decision by the first rule of Chinese bureaucracy: no decision is always better than any decision, including the right decision. Even if they understood the rolling thunder of Milton's sentences, they could rest in the certainty that third-year students wouldn't.

Though I had prefaced, interspersed, and summarized the text of Milton's words with my own cunning elucidation, it turns out that most of them had never heard of censorship and were certain that if it existed, it was only a foreign idea. They certainly had me there. I loved the brilliant simplicity of it: if you effectively censor the concept of censorship, you need not censor anticensorial statements.

It all reminded me of a story another American had told me of coming onto a Dai village so remote that even his local guides were surprised to see it. The villagers were all fixated on a community top-spinning contest (top-spinning is a major-league sport among some of the area's ethnic groups). They were also a bit mellow from chewing betel nut. My friend Conroy wandered about, thinking they were pretty blasé about his presence. He finally asked one red-toothed spectator if strangers had been there before. The man thought it over a minute, then asked, "Are you a stranger?"

Conroy may have just had the bad luck of approaching the village idiot or a guy with a major betel nut habit, but he left that village feeling much the way I felt at the end of that class period: alien beings and alien freedoms are equally unimpressive if you don't know what you're missing.

Tongue Mobilization

Periodically the dean of the foreign languages department would notice that as soon as the students stepped outside the classroom into the hallways and balconies of the building, they spoke only Chinese. The between-class roar that emanated from our building sounded just like the one coming from the science building across the road—pure Chinese. During the ten-minute periods between classes the students relaxed and very naturally resorted to their own language. But the dean felt that English-language students should relax in English. At such times, she and the party secretary would call a department meeting at which she would exhort the students to "mobilize their tongues."

One annual event for tongue mobilization was the English speech contest. Various faculty and students casually informed Mary and me that a speech contest would be held next week. By now we knew this was the Chinese way of saying we were expected to be judges. By now we also were savvy enough to just say, "Ah, very interesting," and play dumb. The three days before the contest were punctuated quite often by designated faculty and students casually mentioning there would be a speech competition and us responding densely, "Ah, very interesting." The morning of the contest, Zhi Xian finally directly asked if we would like to be judges. "Ah, of course we would." Fortunately, they couldn't actually leave the selection of winners only to foreigners, so there were also three Chinese faculty judges (so that proper rhetoric and proper contestants would be rewarded).

In fact, we were never told who won. We eventually found out through department gossip, but there was no formal or ceremonial announcement of winners. The students, both winners and losers, were equally reticent to even mention the competition once it was over. And I don't know, in this case, whether it was more risky to win or to lose.

What I remember most were the tortuously ornate, convoluted phrasings, and the topics, which ran from mundane ("friendship" was a favorite subject) to ideological (celebration of socialist freedoms and scorn for capitalist family structure).

Jameson was one of the contestants. Of all the students in the department, he was the most verbally facile. He had the best comprehension of modern idioms, acquired vocabulary quicker, and simply spoke English more naturally than any of his classmates. Yet, in the contest, he let out my favorite malapropism of the day. His speech was a hilariously misinformed lament in which he piteously described poverty-stricken Americans "living on farewell." He meant "welfare."

Another of my favorites was a speech in which vacationing was described as "making a trip to the beautiful place to kill the time." I think I gave that one high marks. Several contestants craftily praised teachers. One went so far as to proclaim, "The teacher is the engineer of the soul."

The more determined students faithfully listened to both Voice of America and BBC broadcasts. They often heard phrases and idioms that were just too culturally mysterious.

Even the staid old BBC could vastly confuse an English learner. For example, just try to explain how or why a nice woman like Margaret Thatcher could "get in hot water with the back bench." The Easter bunny turned out to be even more inexplicable. A faculty member came across a reference to the Easter bunny and asked for an explanation. Just try to find the key to comprehension regarding a large rabbit that somehow produces pastel eggs. "Do you eat the rabbit?" he asked, sensibly trying for an analogy to the Thanksgiving turkey. I was forced to conclude that I've never understood the Easter bunny.

Student journals were also a rich vein of cultural confusion.

One student bravely and charmingly wrote of attending a Christian church meeting: "We didn't know that only a Christian can eat Jesus' meat and blood. Thank God! When we returned the wine, we got no punishment at all." I was never sure whether she expected punishment from God or the Communist party.

Much of the journal writing was about beautiful sunsets, and the virtue of study, but infrequently it could be stunning in its openness and its feeling, as in this excerpt from a female student's work:

> I wonder why foreigners are always so humor[ous] and our Chinese are just dull. It is because that they have bread as main food while we have rice—I've heard the answer many times when we talk of the differences. In fact, I know, it's the problem of the culture level of the whole nation. But I still doubt. Two thousand years ago, our nation was one of the most developed country of the world, why they didn't pass us some humor? I now know the reason. Every Chinese from his very childhood on, he is taught not to go beyond his bounds, not to think and speak as what actions [happens] to him. How can man's imagination not be inhibited? And that's still the educational system in our country now. That's why our students can pass exams easily but they can't do practice [practical] things so easily.
>
> It's Teacher's Day today. All the teachers in our department are invited to a dinner. I think of my parents. Mother had been a primary school teacher for thirty-five years before she retired last April. She gets what for all her life? She was my class master from the first year to the fifth year in primary school. I knew she loved her students and did her best to help them. Normally a teacher is very proud when he sees his students play roles in every department and every place in his old age. But how about Mother? She went to the countryside with father and the students there don't want so many

[much] knowledge, they're just content with the drab amounts they can tell and several words they can read. And anymore, the teaching conditions there are so bad and sometimes they even don't have money to buy a blackboard eraser. So now, she has worked the whole life for nothing—the money a primary school teacher earns is just enough for himself, and now she even can't be proud of her students.

This was the most honest expression of frustration and sorrow I would encounter in my entire year. When various party functionaries, teachers, and "intellectuals" would blather on to me about "4,000 years of civilization" and "great progress since liberation," I would think of that country teacher who could not be allowed the price of an eraser, and her daughter's anger.

I wrote what I thought might be a note of appreciation on the margins of the journal and returned it to its author, trying to say, as appropriately as I could, that the teacher might be proud of the daughter. But I never mentioned this to anyone else in the department, and she and I never talked about it.

Tough Nuts

The Chinese love aphorisms. This is natural, given the tradition that wisdom is found in the words of a great teacher, whether that teacher be Confucius, Mencius, or Mao. I don't mean that everyone goes around speaking like a fortune cookie (which is an American invention and nonexistent in China) or that the quotations of Chairman Mao are still in vogue. But there seems to be a stock of phrases or sayings that continually pop up in discussion. This is true when the Chinese speak Chinese and perhaps it is a way of simplifying for the foreign listener whose comprehension is as limited as mine. Certainly I appreciated any such verbal shortcuts. However, the use of aphorisms seemed equally attractive to the Chinese when they spoke English. A phrase my students frequently used with great satisfaction was "one more tough nut to crack," whether in reference to examinations or soccer matches. I couldn't think of any literary source for this phrase, nor did it seem likely they acquired it from the speech patterns of a previous teacher. Perhaps there was a closely corresponding Chinese aphorism that reinforced its appearance in their English conversation, but if there was, no one could ever tell me.

Its use in one particular discussion reinforced my view that Chinese thinking is less dualistic than our own and that they naturally and unselfconsciously think of the world as Chinese and nuances of Chinese; not as Chinese and non-Chinese. "One more tough nut to crack" was used by one of the young men of the senior class in reference to Macao, Hong Kong, and Taiwan. This was just after the announcement of the Portuguese/Chinese agreement on the return of Macao to China in 1999. Long before that, details had been worked out by which English governance of Hong Kong would cease in 1997.

My student's response to these two events was to satisfactorily announce, "Only one more tough nut to crack." He meant Taiwan.

Frankly, I had never thought of Macao, Hong Kong, and Taiwan as similar entities, subject to similar resolutions. In the case of Macao, the Portuguese government had years ago voluntarily made the decision to return Macao to China. Only the conditions of transfer were debated. The fate of Hong Kong was ordained by the time frame of the ninety-nine-year agreement that established Hong Kong as a Crown Colony of Great Britain. Whatever deficiencies might be attributed to the English, they do abide by the rule of law.

So to my Western mind, there is a very great difference between the colonies of Macao and Hong Kong and the state of Taiwan—the latter being a Chinese government with its own claim to legitimacy and international sovereignty. If anything, its economic and political autonomy has been strengthened since the withdrawal of U.S. recognition.

In the eyes of the world, Taiwan is a separate political, economic, and national entity historically entangled with, but severed from, the People's Republic of China. But in the eyes of my student, there is only China and its nuances, with Taiwan being, exactly like Macao and Hong Kong, "one more tough nut to crack."

Incidentally, as the 1997 deadline approaches, Hong Kong citizens prepare for the change of government with varying degrees of fatalism. The Chinese government tries to gloss the future with the aphorism "one China, two economies" and with the guarantee that Hong Kong will have the same autonomy as that accorded Tibet. This is cold comfort, especially in light of the uprisings and military response in Tibet in 1987 and 1989.

The Hong Kong poor can only wait and see, while the Hong Kong monied prepare for the worst by shopping for foreign passports and property. Ironically, Taiwan's economy is a major beneficiary of these fears. On July 15, 1987, the *South China Morning Press* (a Hong Kong newspaper) reported a fifty-percent increase in Hong Kong investment in Taiwan over the previous year. Jardine Matheson, one of the oldest and largest trading companies there, speaks confidently of Hong Kong's future while shifting its headquarters to the Caribbean. Rumors circulate about the Hong Kong wealthy buying up estates in Los Angeles and San Francisco. The scramble for passports—Canadian, Australian, even Belizean—is real but not yet as intense as the rumor-mongering about it. A U.S. passport remains the first choice, but as my students might say, "That is a tough nut to crack."

The Party

After a few months of living and teaching with Chinese faculty, one day I realized that although there are continual references to "the party" and to "liberation" (the 1949 culmination of government control by the Communist party) and to "leaders," almost no one ever called themselves or anyone else "Communists." As everyone is supposed to be, maybe it would be redundant to mention it.

Probably they get enough verbal reinforcement during the weekly political study meeting all employees must attend. Every unit or department has its own meeting, presided over by the party secretary or his designate. These meetings are attended with the same gusto that faculty everywhere attend department meetings and, reportedly, are just as productive. They must last a prescribed length of time and often degenerate into napping or reading newspapers.

The party secretary is the guard dog of doctrine. Each department has such a creature, and in turn there is a university party secretary to whom they all report. So, in effect, there is a dual system of administration throughout the institution: department procedure is jointly determined by the department head and the department party secretary; university matters must be jointly agreed to by the president and the university party secretary. The system is ponderous, unproductive, and designed to make any sort of change tortuously slow. I dwell on this because it is how the party maintains control over all institutions. The entire country is administered by a dual bureaucracy of party loyalists and institutional managers. Nothing happens fast; and if it can't be rationalized in party dogma, nothing happens. Foreign businesses who jump into joint ventures usually learn this the hard way.

Mantras

The Han Chinese are the most nonreligious people I've ever encountered. It's very difficult to determine how much of this is the result of Marxist doctrine in early education. However, all the

Chinese I knew of student age were cheerfully contemptuous of religious belief. Jim, one of my graduate students, was friendly with some local Westerners whom he referred to as "quite pious." They were part of a cryptomissionary network that encourages its followers to take teaching positions at Chinese universities.

In Nanning there was a small cell of such English teachers who were very discreetly, very inoffensively Christian. Whenever one of them left a teaching job, he or she could always recommend an equally "pious" replacement to the school. This group wasn't part of any university exchange program like most teaching Westerners. Instead, every one of them I knew was vaguely connected to Hong Kong. They were English, Hong Kong English, or Canadian. They knew and communicated with their counterparts in other Chinese cities and would plan their holidays around visiting and meeting fellow faith-sharers.

Every week the local group would meet for "discussion." If possible, they would include any Chinese student who wanted to practice English. That is as near as they ever came to proselytizing. They just very subtly let their students know that they were Christians and were happy to answer any questions about religion. At the same time, they never imposed their religiosity on the rest of us Westerners and actually avoided the topic in the mixed company of those outside their small group. I never learned the name associated with this network, but I was told by a long-time Western resident of China that the Chinese were aware of such a Hong Kong connection and actually condoned it because it was a steady source of moral, untroublesome English teachers.

At any rate, Jim often attended their meetings, as did a handful of other students. A few decades ago there were "rice Christians": Chinese who used the missionaries as a steady source of food. Jim was sort of the modern equivalent, using these teachers as a conduit to Western culture and English language. He may even have enjoyed their company. But he was blithely immune to religion and seemingly baffled by the very idea. Like all graduate students of English, he was constantly on the lookout for an English book to translate. The subject was almost irrelevant, as long as the book was short. Rather perversely, another teacher recommended *Siddartha,* by Hermann Hesse. Jim tackled it with gusto but immediately encountered some troublesome words and ideas. For instance, "mantra" was beyond his ken. He came to me for clarification. As I began to explain the idea of repeating a sound for the purpose of altering consciousness, he was suddenly holding his sides, roaring with laughter— interspersed with *om*'s, which brought on more laughter. His hilarity was so contagious I started laughing and *om*-ing along with him.

But that was only the edge of the cultural chasm separating Jim from *Siddartha*. It was a shock to me that this very bright, articulate, and studious young man was totally, utterly ignorant of Hindu culture. In my own ignorance, I assumed all Asians were acquainted with one another's ways. Equally impressive was his lack of any religious sensitivity. He found the whole idea hilarious. Fortunately, he soon abandoned the translation. His version of *Siddartha* would have been about as useful as a guide to brain surgery printed in Braille.

However, this same paragon of Marxist Realism and all his fellow graduate students were shockingly superstitious. The most doctrinaire of them told me of his friend, an economics major (and therefore fully immersed in Marxism), who believed in fortune-telling. My student saw the irony of this and was fully amused by it, but also acknowledged his own belief in fortune-telling. This led indirectly into a discussion of ghosts. They were surprised that I didn't believe in ghosts, as they all did. They agreed that Chinese ghosts always had bulging eyes and long teeth, and were unimpressed when I could only describe Western ghosts as rather pale and lifeless.

Somehow their religious indifference seems to leave them vulnerable to superstition; or perhaps it is just the tenuousness of their lives. At any rate, their speech patterns are ripe with references to "luck" and "fortune." "He had no luck at all" is a common phrase. "Bad luck" frequently popped up in all my students' speech and writing as explanation for the outcomes of sports events, grades, travel, or work. Fortune-telling by cards, tea leaves, or the chicken bones after a banquet were common experiences. New Year's prophecies and auspicious signs were taken seriously. But mantras will never catch on.

The Library

Mary had a very useful insight. We foreigners were like the new library rising on campus to the skyscraper height of ten stories: we were to be seen but not efficiently used. In relation to the university's book collection, the new library is about seven floors oversized and will be virtually impossible to maintain. The power demands for controlling temperature and humidity to enhance book life are a cruel joke for a university that can't supply electricity to its teaching and living facilities on a regular basis. The current book collections would break a Western librarian's heart: the spines crack and pages crumble as you open the books; the mildew from their jackets covers your hands. The library staff is thoroughly trained on how to keep books out of the wrong hands (students are strictly limited on which books are available to them) but indifferent to the bacteria and mites that leave little round burrows through the pages.

Modern building maintenance is a concept yet to be learned in this part of China. The large, modern hotels in the major cities always bring in foreign management to train the personnel or even send staff to Hong Kong for training. But the big, new buildings that are not specifically for foreign use are subject to Chinese standards of maintenance, which is to say benign neglect. A new high-rise Bank of China in Nanning was occupied, while construction rubble was still in the hallways of the upper floors. The hallways had never been mopped. Westerners weren't supposed to see these levels, and Chinese wouldn't notice. The equipment and water supply necessary to modern janitorial work would not be available even if the desire to use them were present.

The new library will have the same fate. In fact, before we left, the first two floors were in use while interior construction continued on the upper levels. Students had to have special permission to enter, but bureaucrats and cadres wandered about, thrilled by modernization.

But most important, as far as the eye could see the library towered above its surroundings as a symbol of the university's commitment to education and modernization.

Mary's point was that we were the same sort of symbol. What we did—or whether we did anything—was not so important as our evidencing the university's devotion to learning. Our presence showed that they cared enough to hire a big ticket foreign expert. Mixing pride with a sense of exploitation, they would tell me that I was the highest-paid person in the province. This was true. It was equally true that I was making 50 percent less than my colleagues at Nankai University in Tianjin and that my year's salary was less than 4,000 U.S. dollars; but indeed I was richly rewarded by local standards.

Sometimes, when I considered the way my skills were used, I wondered if I was worth such an emperor's ransom. I was teaching exactly the same sort of classes that all the other foreign teachers at local campuses were, and some of them were American students still working on their B.A. degrees back home. One had an M.A., but none had a doctorate and professorial rank back at their own universities. As I was not allowed to teach my own specialty, they were all as well trained for the work as I was—and in many cases, I'm sure they were better at it. Yet I was paid two or three times as much for the same work. But that was just the point: like the library, I cost more and was proof of the university's seriousness of purpose. I was to be seen at public occasions, banquets, holiday excursions, and celebrations; and when foreign faculties were jointly paraded at such events, by my rank and credentials I was to tower over the others.

It's not as though my wife and I didn't earn our pay: we covered as many class hours as we could bear. Most Chinese faculty taught three or four hours per week. One twenty-five-year-old Chinese teacher once told me that teaching more than four hours would "damage his health." We were asked to teach sixteen and agreed to twelve.

So we earned our keep, but the university administrators had little interest in how our abilities might be better used. Perhaps they knew all too well that the Chinese curriculum is impervious to change or impact, especially by a foreigner in one year. But they did enjoy showing us off.

Group Photographs

Near the end of each semester, all the departments on campus would pause in their routines to pose for formal photographs. Taking photographs is still enough of a novelty in China to be a special experience for most people. Young women all have photo albums of themselves and their friends in special places and times. In all pictures, they pose very carefully to express their pleasure, seriousness of purpose, or deep emotion. On Sundays and holidays you will often see groups of young people or families carefully planning and rehearsing their next picture in front of a flower bed or inspirational statue.

The spontaneous or candid snapshot is unthinkable. Even more mysterious from the Chinese viewpoint is the Western tendency to photograph places or objects without someone standing in front of them. That is an "empty" picture and a baffling waste of film. I think there is a clue to Chinese psychology in this perception that a photograph without at least one person in it is essentially a photo of nothing. A scene without human content is so far outside their experience as to be disturbingly meaningless. Photographs are to record where people have been and what they have accomplished. Thus, formally posed group photographs are the very best kind.

When you look at such a photograph with each person standing straight or sitting erect, looking directly into the camera, and smiling to convey happiness and friendship, there is no indication of the pushing, pulling struggle that resulted in this arrangement. With the students it didn't surprise me that each photograph was preceded by some wrestling, shoving, and feigned embarrassment about who was standing next to whom, and how close. Teenage energy and hormones have to be released.

What amazed me was that the same jostling for position was far more serious among the faculty when they gathered for a group photograph. They would literally push and drag one another to various placements in the group. Then some member who seemed content would suddenly break formation as another's placement upset the composition. It was like watching an especially spooky field of thoroughbred race horses being soothed into the starting gates. Just when they all appeared to be settled down, one would rear up and bolt.

Each photograph required four or five minutes of such rearranging before all were settled into motionless formality. It took me awhile to realize that this was a serious power struggle, with each person jockeying for the position that would convey exactly their perception of their relative importance in the group. Each wanted to claim the status due him, but not a bit more. Each photograph resulted in a permanent statement of who was central to the group and who was peripheral. So men and women, some of advanced years, some of whom had worked together for decades, had to sort out anew each semester the rise and fall of their relative influence in the group. Some by seniority and ability were more certain of their status, but it was all subject to delicate shifts. You could lose face by claiming a position of prominence disproportionate to your actual status. Sometimes shoving someone else too far forward was a good means of self-advancement in the next photo.

THREE

✧ ✧ ✧ ✧ ✧ ✧ ✧

Pains of Socialism,
Joys of Socializing

Health

My second week in Nanning I woke up with a virus, an interesting one. The primary symptoms were a numbness of the left side of my face, immobility of facial muscles, and the inability to close my left eyelid. Ultimately I would be diagnosed as having a severe case of Bell's palsy, which is a blockage of the seventh cranial nerve. At the time, my worst fear was that I had suffered a stroke that was somehow restricted to one side of my face.

You really don't appreciate the simple pleasure of blinking until you lose that motor skill for a few months. Periodically, I had to manually pull down the lid to moisten the eye, and I had to avoid strong sunlight. Eventually I learned to get to sleep while holding my eyelid shut. I think I was also suspected of the "evil eye" as I unblinkingly stared at students while mumbling (my mouth was also affected). The students, already confused by trying to imitate Australian, Canadian, and British accents, were now exposed to spastic American.

Two days later, it was obvious this was not going to clear up overnight, so I agreed to visit the medical college. It is not necessary to abandon all hope when entering a Chinese hospital, but it really helps if you abandon all Western expectations. Even those who practice Western medicine do it in the Chinese manner.

I was ushered through darkened hallways (electric power just can't be wasted on casual lighting) past masked personnel and masked patients to a masked doctor. Even being examined by a physician is a group activity in China. So I, Mary, Conroy, Zhi Xian, and some waiting-room bystanders who had become interested in my case all made our way to the examination room. As two doctors were working there simultaneously, our group filled the room nearly to capacity as we merged with the extended family of a small girl sitting on a tiny stool having her eyes checked (all patients start their examination on a tiny stool). My extended family took up their positions along the wall. Occasionally, a spectator wandered through, looking for the best show.

My masked doctor checked my vision, the interior of my eye, my tongue—all the right stuff. He spent about a half hour conversing with me (via Zhi Xian), with other doctors, with passersby; then he filled two pages of a small notebook with diagnosis. Next, a neurologist was called in. He wore shorts, sandals, long white medical coat, and a two-day beard. He stuck and probed for nerve damage and checked the interior of my eye some more. He confirmed the diagnosis and prescribed antibiotic rinse for the unblinking orb, a ten-day course of megavitamin injections, and cortico-steroids. He also advised acupuncture. (The man obviously believed in needles.) The bedside manner and genuine interest of the doctors and the spectators made this a very human as well as medical experience—not nearly as antiseptic as back home but somehow reassuring.

Receiving my injections at the university infirmary proved to be an equally social event. For several weeks, I received daily injections as my doctors tried to overwhelm my malady with sheer volume of vitamins and drugs. I got a shot in each hip. Never were there fewer than four other people in the room at the time: nurses chatting or warming soup on the hot plate, other patients stoically waiting their turn, friends dropping by. They didn't seem to be disturbed by me dropping my trousers, so why should I be?

The acupuncture was equally communal. As it is prescribed for virtually every malady, the acupuncture rooms of the clinic would usually be filled. I would wait for one of the straw-matted cots to be vacated or for a set of needles, recently plucked from a previous patient, to be sterilized. The initial implanting of the electrified needles is momentarily sensational and focuses the mind wonderfully.

No matter what pattern of needle placement was used on me, the key energy point always tapped was the "tiger's mouth," located between my thumb and forefinger. (It was also the most painful, as there is so much neural circuitry compressed into the hand. Generally the areas of exposed, toughened epidermis require the most effort getting the needles to the proper level of penetration.) A typical formation proceeded from my tiger's mouth up the left forearm, along the left jaw line, above and below my unmoving eyelid, with a few needles in my ear, and sometimes one implanted bull's-eye in my forehead. Depending on the level of voltage, one can imagine being a telegraph key on which a frenzied message is being tapped out about Indians attacking the fort. At higher levels, the facial needles shimmied in my peripheral vision. The ones around my eye made the ceiling of the infirmary look like a film that needed framing. Sometimes I had the sensation that my lip was drawing up over my teeth, though the actual contraction was minimal.

During the first month of this illness, I received about fifty injections (mostly vitamins) and more than fifteen acupuncture treatments. It was not until about the third week that a medical college physician used the Western term "Bell's palsy" to describe my condition; a few days after, I received by mail from the United States the medical encyclopedia description of that condition. I had all the classic symptoms of a severe case. The literature described it as probably of viral origin and said that with proper treatment—cortico-steroids and rest—complete recovery followed in almost all cases but could take months. (I had minor lingering traits a year later.)

I had received an ample dosage of steroids, but rest was impossible. The treatments themselves were wearing me out. Along with Texans, the Chinese believe that "too much ain't enough." Each time I failed to be miraculously cured by my treatment, their disappointment in me was more obvious. Clearly, I was doing something wrong. Drastic measures were required, so I was taken to a traditional Chinese hospital where only acupuncture and herbal medicine were practiced. Here, there was no electrical current attached to the needles; instead, the doctor manually twirled them like tiny drills. This was augmented by Moxa heat treatments. Moxa is an herbal mixture packed into cigarlike sticks. Like a good cigar, Moxa holds a long white ash as it burns. This burning tip would be held near to, but not touching, my face. The heat from this was supposed to be beneficial. The gray fumes that wafted above my face were certainly relaxing. It smelled like nothing so much as *cannabis*.

Various hemps, of course, grow wild throughout the countryside, and I am certain that the medicinal herbal mixture called Moxa has a high *cannabis* content. A few needles in the face seemed a very small thing so long as I breathed deeply. But after a month or so, even this lost its thrill. I just wanted to rest. My face was sore; I began to feel like I was taking a beating instead of a treatment. All my Chinese friends remained convinced that more treatment would produce a cure. Their theory of medicine was firmly based on overwhelming the malady with massive force. My illness and unwillingness to recover was becoming a political issue as much as a medical problem. So, even though I still resembled the Phantom of the Opera, I declared myself miraculously cured and stopped all treatment. It was evident by their reactions they considered me mentally unstable for quitting treatment, socially reckless for abandoning them in this community effort, and morally deficient for not responding to time-honored cures. I cheerfully accepted this diagnosis.

Banquets

Early in the first semester, we were hosted by the regional government's deputy secretary-general, who invited the foreign English-teaching faculty to a banquet. The entire menu was minority dishes—unexplored territory even for most of the Chinese present.

It began with Zhuang tea. This required a fellow, dressed like Santa's helper, to drag a red-hot charcoal pot across the carpeting of the private dining room. (This was on the thirteenth floor—thirteen is not a Chinese superstition—of the Nanning Hotel. I started thinking of *The Towering Inferno*, but it turned out I was just another American worrier.) He burned some tea leaves in an iron skillet, pulverizing them with a wooden mallet. These were cooked in oil, then steeped in spiced rice water. The custom is to drink three cups. It was explained that, like the best of lives, the first cup would be bitter, the second sweet, and the third soft and mellow. It worked for me.

Then we settled down to eat everything that had ever slithered or crawled. If it locomoted by gyrating its abdominal section, it was grist for our culinary mill. There was snake, of course; but then, on to eels, various snails, and something that could translate only as "it crawls in water." Apparently, this had been crushed to death by the sheer weight of seasonings, then hacked into unrecognizability. I still wanted to smack mine with a beer bottle before I ate it but instead swallowed quickly. There were also some dishes that can only be described as amazing visual art forms. One platter was a phoenix of startling plumage. Our resident photographer, Mr. Zhiow, stood on his chair and photographed this dish. All this cuisine impressed the locals as much as the foreigners.

There was the usual reign of terror created by constant toasting with no-lead rice wine. The Chinese cannot resist the words or bravura of "bottoms up." I think Mr. Zhiow once toasted out of his lens cap. His potentencyship, the deputy secretary-general, could have been a Chicago alderman; a real political pro, he was alarmingly attentive to me on our three occasions of breaking bread. He said he was "very moved" by a speech I gave at the evening National Day banquet. As it was undoubtedly mangled by the translator, I may have said something quite radical. At any rate, he insisted on sending a car the following week to take me to "the best acupuncturist in Nanning." (Thus did my experience and fame as a reluctant medical patient grow.)

It is worth remembering that at such occasions the benign and magnanimous hosts surrounding us at the banquet tables were all survivors of the Cultural Revolution, a harrowing time. In 1986–87, they had begun to feel a bit expansive as the economic and foreign policy of China became relatively enlightened. Now, in mellow moments as banquets ended with sated appetites and ebullient fellowship, they jokingly, wistfully fantasized American and Australian travel junkets for themselves. In truth, nothing could have better served China than for more of its best leadership to have experienced other worlds. Even ours.

Art and Entertainment

Nanning is to culture as file cabinets are to computers, so a touring ballet company from Beijing was periodically sent in the same spirit that food is sent to famine areas. Both hoi polloi and nouveau-cultured were present at the performance we attended. At the Nanning Theater, it's strictly find-your-own-seat, but unlike Chinese trains and planes, the ballet starts on time. So with the room filling and the crowd milling, the lights went out and it was showtime!

A pretty lady in a "senorita gown" announced the first and all subsequent dances. As the crowd was climbing over seats and settling into the aisle, an almost laughable Spanish heel-clicking number was offered. It looked like a long evening.

But this had been merely a throwaway to get the crowd's attention. Things improved steadily. The Chinese senorita was back in a jiffy. A short folk dance was followed by several more of the same, then a pleasantly erotic modern piece that was daring by Chinese standards. One of our companions, Qing Mai, was relieved that the audience did not hoot, howl, and yell lurid suggestions. The local gentry were just becoming accustomed to nonparticipatory theater. The program also contained two selections from *Swan Lake*. Actually, most of the female dancers were quite good, and, not as anorexic as Western dancers, they were also a bit of all right. Someone had had the good sense to choreograph most of the dances so that the males just ambled about and caught the odd flying female or swan. (Chinese male dancers are button-cute but balletically untrained.) The hit of the evening, however, was the Cultural Revolution classic, *The Woman In Red*. Even its announcement brought enthusiasm from the audience, who responded to the characters like old friends. Qing Mai later explained this was because during the Cultural Revolution the only film seen for years every week at the Saturday night movies was *The Woman In Red*. Whether they were still entranced by the Revolutionary theme or responding to familiar clichés, like our *Rocky Horror Picture Show* audiences, was unclear. But it had stirring, rousing music and was well danced.

If Wagner had been Chinese, his Valkyries would have worn red pajamas. The story is set on Hainan Island. A spunky peasant girl has defied the evil intents of the evil landlord. She is hunted in the forest by a pack of evil henchmen. They find her, and with the evil landlord leering, they beat her and leave her in the forest. It is a dark and stormy night. She survives through spunk. She is found by Communist rebels (easily identified by the type of automatic pistol they carried—the audience applauded the pistols). She falls in love with the equally pretty, equally spunky party secretary. They capture the evil landlord, but through evil, he somehow gets away. Then the evil landlord captures the spunky, pretty party secretary and burns him at the stake. The spunky peasant girl is galvanized into a fearless Revolutionary leader. Lots of cheering.

Chinese films, while thematically not daring, are cinematically well done and interesting, although we understood about one in fifteen words of the dialogue. The aforementioned Saturday night movies are shown outdoors in sports arenas. It's sort of like going to the drive-in without your car. On campus, literally thousands of people carry their chairs to the athletic stadium. This goes on all winter (which, there, means a damp 40 degrees). Along with chairs, people bring coats, blankets (actually it might be a lot more fun for the sexually repressed youths in the winter), and umbrellas for watching in the rain.

Mail

Zhi Xian stopped by one afternoon. He seemed to have no particular agenda but mentioned in an offhand manner that there was a package at the railway station downtown that was perhaps of interest to a foreigner. The Foreign Affairs Office had so informed him. It was from the United States and addressed to Guangxi University but to no particular person. So naturally it was being held at the rail station as unclaimed and accruing daily fees. The fee was only a few *fen* (pennies) per day, but of course this could go on indefinitely. Picking it up would require someone making a decision and risking public funds for perhaps the wrong purpose.

Unless, of course, a reckless foreigner took the bull by the horns. Given this reckless foreigner's lust for mail, any mail, nothing more need be said. Zhi Xian had done his Chinese number, and now his conscience was clear and his expression properly blank.

It was a miserably humid day when I did the four-mile bike trip. Yes, the foreigner could have the package if he paid the fees due and had the proper notice of the package (a three-by-five-inch onionskin paper with the red seals of officialdom stamped all over it). Yes, the Foreign Affairs Office was happy to entrust that to me when I had bicycled back to campus. What a good joke that I was so foolish as to try to pick up a package without papers. Sixteen miles later, after my second journey to the rail station, I returned to the university in sweaty triumph with a packet of graduate program bulletins from the U.S.A. for a Chinese student looking for a ticket out of the asylum.

Free Conversation

Without warning, or at least on very short notice, our Chinese hosts often would spring a "show-and-tell" event on us. We were simply told that a car would be sent in an hour to take us to a public event at which we would be paraded before the bureaucrats of other schools and government agencies as indicators of our university's commitment to modernization. We would be expected to sip tea, eat seeds, smoke incessantly, listen to prolonged clichés, and then briefly voice reciprocating clichés of modernization and cultural friendship. It's the sort of thing you must get used to as a foreign guest. It was annoying only when you had plans that had to be abandoned, as no personal appointment could override official events, even when no advance notice was given. Every foreigner in China has had this experience of

The egg lady, Nanning free market

Four generations in a Guangxi village

A bird fancier and his caged friends

Pack mules carrying supplies along the Great Wall

suddenly being given an invitation you can't refuse. It goes with the territory.

Sometimes the Chinese even surprise one another. One such example occurred toward the end of the first semester. It seems that the previous year, in the height of the new sense of intellectual freedom that at first accompanied the economic reform policies, a day had been organized for all the foreign and Chinese intellectuals to meet. This was a fairly radical concept, but it must have gone off well because it was to be repeated. Those foreigners who had been in Nanning the previous year said it was a surprisingly loose, casual affair. However, only a few days before the scheduled repeat performance, the student demonstrations of 1986 had begun in other Chinese cities, especially Shanghai.

It would have been too great a reaction to cancel at that point, but an alternative to open conversation was clearly needed. The result was one of the strangest gatherings I attended in China. We foreigners, all thirty or so of us, were collected from the various campuses at 8:00 A.M. and bused to a meeting hall at the museum. There, while serving attendants poured hot water into our teacups, we were seated at long tables amply supplied with seeds, citrus, and cigarettes. The TV cameras and lights slowly scanned our foreign faces as we sipped, smoked, spit seed shells, and tried to figure out what was going on. Official speeches and clichés by party leaders lasted about an hour; then we were told we could have a half hour of "free conversation."

Thirty minutes later (more than enough time for the TV cameras to record the entire crowd and show free intellectual discussion on the evening news), while we were still trying to digest seeds and significance, all the lights were turned off for a movie—a Chinese-made cop show. Its title, translated, was something like *Action Beyond Boundaries*. Basically it was a Chinese version of *Day of the Jackal*, all about high-tech police surveillance combating and ultimately defeating high-tech assassination. A key bit of dialogue included the line, "China will not be a platform for terrorism." This was spoken by the protagonist, a highly professional, highly efficient, highly conscientious, highly overworked Beijing police commander. The Chinese are very competent filmmakers, but this was a turgid, plodding mess that lovingly displayed computers, TV screens, surveillance equipment, helicopters, and lots of telephones. There were more phones in this film than in Beijing; the overworked cop was always shown taking a phone call while signing stacks of official documents.

Though foreign influence was the source of evil in the plot, foreign imports and consumer items were lingered over as signs of modernization. Lots of foreign cigarettes and the foreign contents of snap-top cans were consumed by the harried good guys. The serene good girls all wore the sweater sets and plaid skirts that were then the fashion rage among the Beijing smart set. Inadvertently, the film displayed the deeply felt ambiguity the Chinese have toward the West and its culture: our technology is useful; our culture is decadent; and both are so damned irresistible. So of course it will require the best efforts of China's higher civilization to absorb the technology and spit out all the immorality.

Then the lights came on and the meeting was over with the abruptness that characterizes every Chinese event, and we all got back on the bus.

Friendship Stores

The size of a Friendship Store (and the volume of merchandise therein) varies directly with the number of tourists visiting each city. Beijing has the largest: a four- or five-story giant just down the street from the Jianguo Hotel and the other major tourist havens. (It is also very near the best money-changing area in Beijing, but that is another topic.)

At the other end of the continuum, there is the Nanning Friendship Store. Remember, there were less than thirty of us resident foreigners in Nanning—plus an occasional tourist who took the wrong train from Guilin, or thought Nanning was Nanking, or was visiting one of us.

So our Friendship Store was one of the shabbiest of the lot, though probably more representative of the system than the Beijing store. The name was a cruel joke, perhaps the only example of a flair for dark comedy to be found in China. I began to think of it as a *gulag* for government employees who distinguished themselves in surliness and customer avoidance.

As these two traits are the normal attitude of clerks in Friendship Stores, I coined a new diagnostic category to describe the Nanning clerks: "aggressive catatonics." Of course, this sounds like bigotry and racism to anyone who has never had to shop for the staples of life in China's government-run stores, but it is accurate. The behavior of the clerks is due partly to the "iron rice bowl" syndrome and partly to the low status associated with jobs that serve the public rather than the glorious Revolution.

The "iron rice bowl" refers to the lifetime employment guaranteed in a government job. That is the good news and the bad news. The job is yours forever. You have the comfort and the horror of knowing that you can sit on the same stool forever, watching the merchandise fade in the sunlight, whether you ever make a sale or not. (In October 1986, Deng Xiaoping made an effort to put at least a dent in the iron rice bowl, naming it a major barrier to the Four Modernizations, but to almost no effect since then.) As you might suspect, everyone deplores the other guy's iron rice bowl and feverishly defends his own.

The malaise is compounded by the traditional perception of shop clerk as a servile position. Being a servant is anti-Marxist and antirevolutionary, in spite of the paradox that every successful revolution results in a bureaucracy comprised primarily of servile toadies. However, the Communist bureaucrat can still hold up the veil of "service to the Revolution." When your job is clearly and simply service to the guy who wants to buy a roll of toilet paper, it's harder to maintain any revolutionary illusions. Worse yet, in the poorly stocked stores the customer is very likely to want something you don't have, and such a situation is loaded with potential loss of face.

Getting a clerk to acknowledge you requires entrapping them: the surest tactic is to sneak up when they are asleep with their heads on the counter—a very common clerking posture. (Again, you think I exaggerate.) Once so snared, the clerk is then forced to pick up an inventory pad with several layers of carbon and make some sort of running inventory on the futile pretense of keeping the shelves stocked. Or perhaps they are required to explain every purchase they cannot avoid or prevent. I have actually tried to buy displayed items only to be told that selling them is not allowed—because, if the item were sold, it couldn't be seen as evidence of modernization.

The highly skilled, educated foreign professionals who come to live in China as carriers and models of urban-industrial modernization soon are reduced to the level of hunters and gatherers in their personal lives. We all became foragers, spending hours of each day seeking out the staples of life. I experienced deep satisfaction, even accomplishment, in finally running to ground a few containers of peanut butter. I carefully carried a jar of mustard from Beijing to Nanning. I was truly thrilled to finally locate rolls of toilet paper next to the fireworks in the free market. To the Western mind, there may be no apparent logic by which goods are shelved; you wouldn't expect the butter to be stocked in the cigarette case, but there it is.

When the foreigners get together, at least half the conversation is food centered—who has last seen what, and where, and might it still be there? Some of our group could become unhealthily aroused at the subject of chocolate. They would have husky-voiced conversations about chocolate experiences in their past—their first chocolate, Dutch chocolate versus English chocolate, and crazy weekend chocolate binges that ended badly.

Foreign Aid

Within the small circle of local foreigners, the Australian foresters and their families held a prominent place in the social hierarchy. In large part, this was simply because they were amiable, pleasant company and generous hosts. In their genuine friendliness, the Australian stereotype of open, easy camaraderie was perfectly exemplified. However, some of their social standing was due to the fact that they had a higher standard of living than the rest of us. As they were employed by the Australian government (the reforestation work was an Australian foreign aid project), they received monthly supplies of food and creature comforts from home. So their parties and dinners were as near as the rest of us got to home-style celebrations.

One example was a Sunday gathering at the forestry compound about twenty kilometers outside Nanning. The burning of meat in the backyard is a tradition as sacred to the Aussies as to any segment of the American population, be it southern or suburban. So to introduce Lester and Julie (the latest forester couple to arrive) we surviving Westerners, including two Japanese, were invited for a "barby"—which in this case was not the long-legged object of Ken's extruded plastic lust, but hamburgers and pork filets scorched on grills of welded plow discs. There was a delicious blend of matey talk, spiced by Japanese *r*-free English, long *o*'s from Canada, midwestern twangs, and the singsong "brrs" of a Hong Kong Scot. Of course, several cases of Castlemain Export Lager added to both the accents and the ambience. (For awhile, I thought I might have to be taken away in an ambience.)

Even when the cricket pitch was set up, the decorum did not improve. Not a white flannel in the field. A ten-year-old won batting honors, retiring with the agreed maximum of twenty-five runs. I salvaged what reputation I could with two runs, damned pleased to not be shut out or seriously injured by the ten-year-old's younger brother, who was hurling rockets at the wicket I was defending with my body and bat. The hardest thing about cricket is learning to carry the bat while running: it means leaving your Castlemain dangerously unguarded at the wicket.

The cricket match ambled through the afternoon—an amiable, chatty, boozy sort of game with no end in sight. As in the best English matches, play was suspended for tea, and never resumed due to gluttony (tea being cheesecakes, a chocolate cake, coffee, and more Castlemains). The day was a lovely processional of good talk, good food, good cheer, and good company. It started midmorning, and the first time I looked at my watch it was 7:30 P.M. Everyone's Monday morning began to assert itself—all work days start senselessly early in south China (you'd think something would get done). One more Castlemain, another round of conversational clusters, lingering at the van, handshaking all around, a Chinese driver being obviously patient as only the Chinese can be obviously patient, more lingering, then we entered the van and reentered China.

The Fork versus Chopsticks

Before coming to China, it was my long-cherished prejudice that the only worthwhile achievements in the last 10,000 years of human history were hot water and the ice cube. I really think anyone is on shaky ground who would oppose this view by mentioning such things as religion or art or democracy.

Everyone, other than fanatics who use water only for baptisms or for restraining lust, must admit that water, glorious water, water piping hot or chilled to crystalline form, has done more to increase human happiness than any of the extortionist tactics, insults, and threats to human intelligence written in the name of religiosity. Controlling the temperature of water from boiling to freezing is the single advance in human history that is an unqualified success—adding not one cubit to suffering, while increasing pleasure exponentially. The same cannot be said, even of the arts—performing or visual or written. The mere mention of klezmer music or New Expressionism or Samuel Taylor Coleridge attests to my view. As for the benefits of democracy, I need write only two words: Ronald Reagan. Hot water and ice cubes are unquestionably the achievements worth salvaging and treasuring from the rubbish bin called civilization.

My year in China, a land that hasn't quite got the knack of either, did nothing to weaken this prejudice. However, travel is broadening; so I have expanded my cultural horizons, adding one more item to my list: the fork.

Prior to arrival in China, I was one of those soft-headed, bleeding-heart liberals who thought that such things as the relative merits of the fork and chopsticks should go unjudged and simply be recognized as cultural differences, implying no degree of better or worse. Before coming to China, I happily practiced with chopsticks, learning to pick up dumplings, cubed meat, sprouts, tofu, and even paper clips. (I was diligent and determined to not disgrace or deprive myself.)

This training served me well; I can get nearly every grain of rice from my bowl. As I have been told that each rice grain represents a bead of sweat from the peasant's brow, I try to leave my bowl sweat-free. So it is not as though I can't manage to feed myself with the sticks. In fact, I can pick up the solitary peanut at the banquet table. It's the pigeon eggs that are the slipperiest, and even with them I can acquit myself with trencherman's honor.

So my bias toward the fork is not based on inability to gain nourishment with the sticks. Rather, I shower the fork with accolades because it allows one noise-free eating without splashing or slurping. The chopstick fancier must feverishly slurp and shovel at the breakfast bowl of congee. The vacuuming technique is necessary to efficiently process rice or long noodles. The hollow-stemmed vegetables that are the green staple of south China's nutrition must also be simultaneously sucked and gnawed, which often leaves a dew about the cheeks and chin; and this precipitation is no respecter of adjacent diners or their bowls.

The other incontestable advantage of the fork is that it is often accompanied by a knife. This allows one to cut tough meat or long-stemmed vegetables or spring rolls or steamed buns into pieces of a size that can be completely inserted into the mouth, thereby allowing one to close the lips while chewing. Then one does not have to lean over the bowl with teeth around one end of the morsel in question, chopsticks pulling on the other end, like a pair of terriers tugging on a shared rat.

The fork-and-knife combination also allows the diner to bone the meat before placing it in the mouth, which eliminates the necessity of spitting the bones onto the table or floor.

In brief, the fork affords less noise, less splash, and less spitting, and greatly reduces the danger of choking to death on tough, stringy, outsized edibles. It earns its position on the short list of civility, right below hot water and the ice cube.

FOUR

Street Scenes

Dying Guys Don't Beg

I found myself looking for the dying guy as I threaded my way along Yellow Street. (Not its actual name, this was the street I took to the only bakery in town that sold an approximation of French bread. I had dubbed it "Yellow Street" because of the tiles that cover the storefronts and because of the hepatitis evident in the vendors' eyes.) Anyway, the dying guy wasn't in his usual spot. I didn't know if he had finished dying or if someone had moved him.

Every shopping area of every Chinese city has at least one dying guy. I don't mean a beggar. (Dying guys don't beg; if you tossed your traveler's checks at a dying guy, he still wouldn't move.) Up the block, Yellow Street has a beggar. Blind, he sits barefoot with his cane and his bowl in the middle of the street, a human traffic island, with pony carts, bicycles, motorcycles, trucks, and pedestrians dividing and flowing past on either side of him. He has a dignified, low-key begging style—he just sits there in traffic and lets you make your own decision. But if you tossed your traveler's checks into his bowl, he would do the right thing. He's a beggar, not yet fixed on becoming a dying guy.

But I don't think even dying guys are fixed on being that when they lie down for the final time, or surely they would pick their spots with a little more care: someplace a little quieter or warmer (dying must be cold) or with some ambience. But the dying guys I saw were just hunkered down on busy sidewalks, exposed to heat, cold, sun, rain, trash, and human indifference. I think they settle on a curb thinking it's just a rest stop, and then experience a total absence of will when it's time to get up. Their bodies look no worse than those of the beggars or even a lot of pedestrians passing by. It's the will—the will to rise and endure another round of degradation—that vacates the body and leaves a man immobilized on the sidewalk. The old will just says, "To hell with this. I'm gonna get some dignity."

So a dying guy will occupy the same little piece of pavement for days, not moving. His eyes don't try to make contact; you don't have to worry about him trying to hassle you or embarrass you or shake you down. He doesn't want anything, not even another minute. You pass him a few days in a row and then, just when you start looking for him, he's gone. You can't count on anybody these days.

Roadside

It's the men and women squatting by the roadside who keep this country going. On every trafficked street there are repairmen, each one a specialist, who fix shoes, bikes, zippers, leather goods, or pots and pans.

The entire country should be turned into a shoe repair shop. China could import shiploads of shoes needing heels and half soles, fix them, and still get them back to us faster than our neighborhood shoe repair shops. Everything is fixed while you squat on a brick-sized stool. If it's a major overhaul, you may have to return a few hours later, but it'll be fixed in some fashion. Inventories are ugly scraps of rubber, leather, and canvas sailcloth from which repairmen can fashion heels, soles, and patches for all styles and conditions. What can't be glued is stitched with a treadle sewing machine. Along with bicycle repair, it's the best service in China.

The bicycle repair guys patch inner tubes of the same thickness as surgical gloves. They patch the patches. They fashion wheel spokes from bailing wire. They sort through a startling collection of screws, bolts, and nuts and reconstruct a disintegrated pedal. They have bicycle pumps, which for three fen you can use to reinflate your leaky tires enough to get to the market and back. Sometimes air is "on the house."

Like all the street repair people, they calmly solve any problem working from a piteously inadequate toolbox. Their solution is always a Band-Aid instead of major surgery—temporary but adequate to get you through the day. They patiently squat beside the street, certain that something will soon break down in front of them. By waiting, they will earn one or two yuan, enough to get them through the day. In spite of all the glorious joint ventures reported in *Beijing Review* and *People's Daily*, it is this Band-Aid economy that still sustains the vast majority of Chinese.

Sleep

Chinese can and do sleep anywhere. On the worst buses, without shock absorbers, traversing the most potholed streets, they put their heads and arms on the nearest seatback and are unconscious in minutes, in postures and conditions that should guarantee whiplash. They can sleep on piles of construction brick, at curbside on the busiest street, in moving trucks atop a load of logs.

This skill is first acquired in infancy; strapped to their mothers' backs, they learn to sleep in spite of her movements. As infants they sleep in bamboo bicycle seats fitted in front of their parent's seat. Some bicycles are equipped with a small headrest between the handlebars. The child will lean into the headrest and softly snore through the journey.

I do not mean that the Chinese sleep instead of working. To the contrary, they work long and devotedly at their tasks. But they also seem to switch off as completely as their machinery when not involved with a task. My theory is that sleep is the only real break possible in the noise, congestion, and sensory overload that is normal in the streets and work places. When they are asleep, they are not in China. This was true of my own night's sleep, which became my major refuge.

The paradox of this public sleeping was that someone seemed to be awake at every hour in our housing complex. The air was continuously filled with the sounds of conversation, arguments, television, sweeping, water filling washtubs, and so forth, at all hours. I don't know if families slept in shifts due to crowding, or if insomnia was epidemic, or if some were only able to sleep while on the street; but someone was always awake.

At home in America, I could never sleep under these conditions because there I would consider the noise a rude, thoughtless invasion of my privacy that I should do something about. In China, it was still a thoughtless invasion of my privacy, but it wasn't rude because actual privacy is inconceivable. There was no alternative to the prevailing conditions. Once I realized this, I was able to sleep through the night. I had no desire to sleep on buses or piles of bricks, but I learned that when you're asleep you're not in China—the noise, odors, and congestion that are China. My sleep became a deep, almost trancelike state. I dredged up memories buried since childhood. Faces and names of grade school chums lost to memory for decades began to visit me in the night.

Beasts of the Fields

One Saturday, Mary and Mrs. Wang climbed onto a bus, competing for space with baskets of chickens and ducks, bundles of sugarcane, and country folk. Mrs. Wang was Mary's painting teacher and also a sort of organizer of local craft production. They were going to Bingian, a textile village, to spend the weekend visiting mills and shops where minority textile items were made and marketed.

So Conroy and I took a hike into the countryside beyond Nanning. The fields ranged from acres of rice and sugarcane and pineapple to bathroom-sized patches of green vegetables. Papaya trees edged the rice paddies or were planted in their own groves. The air was ripe with the smell of centuries of harvest and habitation. It was as quiet as Amish farmland for the same reason— no motorized equipment.

There, even the water buffalo stared at us. These were not sophisticated urban water buffalo who are accustomed to bikes, pony carts, cars, and trucks. These were water buffalo who knew the touch, sight, sound, and smell of about fifty local peasants who walk beside them, lean against them, and swim the stream with them. We were two foul-smelling, white aliens who could not make soothing sounds—a major water-buffalo brain overload.

The peasants giggled and observed from a socially appropriate distance. They would have found a charge uproariously amusing—not due to maliciousness, but because it would have been a wonderful entertainment where otherwise there is none.

The communication between water buffalo and their owners seems total. By voice command, small children and old women move the beasts at will. It may be a complete meeting of minds, in the sense that there must be a selection process (natural or otherwise) whereby those peasants with any imagination or creativity, labeled as dissidents or degenerates, either flee of their own accord or are driven from the countryside. Only those void of the burden of second guesses or deep abstraction could live through days that duplicate one another perfectly, blurring into generations of lifetimes before and after them.

So the beasts and their masters seem perfect mental comple-ments to one another. I say this intending no insult to either. They are, by design and selection, perfect for the lives that are theirs without choice.

The more I observe water buffalo, the more lovely and noble they become. They appear soulful, serious of purpose, thor-oughly reasonable at all times, even with their ears laid back and nostrils flared to sniff repellent white devils who dare to invade water-buffalo paradise.

Interspecies relationships is a subject I had to come around to sooner or later. I missed my dogs and cats. I pressed them from my conscious mind before I slept, and dreamt of them as I awakened. This has always been a character flaw or mild neurosis of mine: to have too many pets and to empathize too much with the damn things (what Erich Fromm in his lovely European English called "a socially patterned defect").

Still, I am only a slightly grotesque exaggeration of what I observe to be a fairly universal tendency. Very simply, other crea-tures give us comfort, ask little, tolerate much, and offer beauty in their form, movement, and sound. Beyond that, they (aside from cats) have been bred into such states of dependency that caring for them may be the only moral responsibility left that most of us are competent to fulfill.

Even in China, where things are tight and the comfort zone has tiny margins, there are the exceptional but all the more poi-gnant examples of interspecies bonds.

A minority group of Western Yunnan called the Na-Khi have their origins in Tibet. They are described by J.F.C. Rock (of whom more later) as practitioners of the most nearly pure form of Bon, the pre-Buddhist animism of Tibet. The remaining texts of their funeral ceremonies describe a special ceremony for the funerals of favorite dogs.

In today's China, in the worst heat of midday, old men bring their caged birds to shady corners of the parks. The birds sit cage by cage and sing—probably gossiping over the relative merits of perches and seeds. Like flyfishers casting their lines, the old men effortlessly arc their specimen nets over the tops of weeds and bushes to catch the odd grasshopper for a bird banquet. Then the old men sit silently, pleased in their power to please their friends who live in smaller cages than their own. I didn't recognize the birds. They are loud and raucous, probably the national bird.

A sign of advancing affluence: at corner street markets, there are areas where tiny goldfish and other decorative miniature fish are displayed in washpans. They are too small to eat, can't scare a burglar, and utterly without intrinsic value. They are just to look at and take care of. They are for peasants and workers who, after ten to twelve hours of labor, want to feel the luxury of being able to care for something for no possible reason but altruism and pleasure.

The Chinese family of five, maybe six, who lived below and across the courtyard from us had a cat named Mee. Mee was a working cat who slugged it out with rats; in return, Mee got tiny but regular feedings and was petted and called by name. Who could ask for more? The same was true of the other two or three cats in our building complex.

The man who lived below us put his chickens away at night with a soothing manner that was more than proprietary. (Okay, he probably ate them when they quit laying, but leave me some illusions.)

I even grew fond of the lizards that lived in the bathroom and on our bedroom screens. The Chinese call them "wall tigers." Mosquito eaters, they remained only associates and cohabitants, not friends.

Yet, instances of casual cruelty toward animals were always evident and always appalled me. (It would have been a sure sign I'd been there too long if they had not.) A tormented monkey on a leash, wearing baby clothes, being listlessly whipped by his young boy master, still would not cavort, jump, or in any way perform for the few fen that the child hoped to collect from passers-by. The monkey's face was like a Goya sketch. I don't know what facial skin coloring a monkey should have, but this one looked sick beyond description. The silence of the monkey and the child was stunning. The boy sat crosslegged, wordlessly taunting the monkey with the small rope whip, almost without expectation of results. The monkey noiselessly expressed the pain, humiliation, and defeat of a prizefighter out on his feet but somehow still vertical. The boy, his grizzled old fight manager, hunched in the corner knowing he had to send his fighter out for one more beating if either of them were to eat again. Both of them were trapped in a sickening attempt to entertain the rest of humanity by brutalizing a life.

Red Eyes

"The ones with the red eyes are the most beautiful," Qing Mai told me as she bought a greeting card resplendent with blue sky, green meadow, and a white angora rabbit. Her rabbit had dark eyes, an aesthetic flaw that caused enormous deliberation over the purchase. Finally, the overall composition of her card won out over the red-eyed bunnies, not so well posed, on other cards. The approaching new year (1987) was the Year of the Rabbit. Chinese merchandisers, like their American counterparts, believe it impossible to sell anything before its time. Therefore, bunny images were reproducing as fast as the real thing in downtown Nanning's shops.

(Some Yankee trader should open a Hallmark card shop in

China. Joyce Hall should be designing a billion National Day cards and New Year's cards right now. No image is too sentimental or too maudlin. At first, I thought all the fluffy kitty images were for tourists. But no; the kittens on cards, towels, posters, clothing, and caps outnumber the tourists. Unless there is an underground kitten cult, this points to a sentimentality that has no other vehicle of expression in the realities of people's lives.)

"Red eyes are more beautiful," Qing Mai repeated for my foreign fuzzy-mindedness. "In that case, I must be strikingly beautiful today," I said, lowering my dark glasses and flashing my crimson orb, still blinkless from the Bell's palsy.

We shared a giggle. China is a great place for a giggler. Chinese giggle at both the mildly amusing and the utterly appalling. My theory is that it is a natural reaction of uncertainty to astounding everyday sights and events that may prove calamitous or inconsequential. It's a reaction perhaps reinforced during the Cultural Revolution, when people were likely to witness horrors and not know if the proper, politically acceptable response was to approve or condemn. Under such conditions a giggle was the safest and most natural stress reliever. So giggle. It's easy to share a giggle, even when it is originating in very different emotions.

Fashion

Nanning is about 26 degrees off the equator; if you follow this line of latitude around the globe you come to places like Havana, Cuba. So, by North American standards, it never has cold weather, although January through March it can be a wet 40 degrees in the evenings and early morning. During this winter, the locals put on long underwear. Their long johns are actually thin, polyester athletic suits—vivid blues, greens, and day-glo pastels in various combinations—they love to wear for almost any occasion. For winter, they simply wear them under their usual clothes. As they are loose-fitting, they tend to stick out of pant legs and shirttails and peek over neckties. No one thinks anything of this.

The only thing I thought odd was that I often still saw the telltale underwear in late May, when the temperature climbed into the humid high eighties.

Another striking sartorial feature among Western-dressed south China males were their belts, which seemed to be in no way related to waist size. Maybe there is only one belt size in China—size 48. The result for the typical slim-waisted Chinese male was that after buckling up, his belt would wrap around almost to the middle of his back. Sometimes you could observe the end of a belt sticking out of the rear vent of a suit jacket. Either they are optimistic about gaining a great deal of weight, or they buy extra long in order to get their money's worth. (They probably figured I was wearing a belt from my childhood, as it ended abruptly a few inches past the buckle. They were discreet enough to never ask.)

Great Expectorations

What do American baseball players and one-fourth of the world's population have in common? An inordinate need to spit. For ballplayers, chewing and spitting is a ritual labor that symbolizes their seriousness of purpose and involvement in the cause shared by their fellow spitters. Like pipe, cigar, or cigarette smokers fondling their apparatus, it gives them something to do, a way to appear thoughtful when accosted with conversation by non-ballplayers. All this can be understood. Surely there are even now being prepared dissertations in sports psychology on topics like "The Self-Actualization of the Cheek Cud."

But what explains the Chinese compulsion to spit, hack, snort, wheeze, and vacuum the sinuses in search of expectorant?

From the vantage point of my Chinese tenement, I could attest to the morning purge of the throat passage. (The collective sound and fury of it made me suspect that what Hercule Poirot calls "the little grey cells" were also being expelled.) The "Do Not Spit" signs drip with cheerful Chinese contempt. Interestingly, these are virtually the only signs printed in both Chinese and English.

Men do it perhaps more than women. But then, in most cultures men excel in displays of wretched excess, whether it be drinking, athletics, or working for money. So, in China they excel in spitting—in frequency, duration, volume, and aeroballistics. But it cannot be written off as Chinese machismo; the ladies are quite well represented in saliva slinging. Even children do it: I wondered at what age a drool becomes a slobber and then metamorphoses into the full-blown *thwack* of a well-tempered spitwad. Spitting is as ubiquitous as bike riding, and the two together in crowds are only for the stout of heart and strong of constitution.

Is it the climate? But the Chinese climate is as variable as that of any sizeable nation. And non-Chinese reside here for years yet remain only casual spitters.

Does it have to do with the Chinese concept of body cleanliness? I suspect so. There is the paradox, of course, that the liquid litter that polka-dots the ground and pavement is a major reason colds and throat infections are never absent from the community, linger in the sufferers for months, and periodically reach epidemic proportion in every classroom and work place (yes, Chinese spit in the classroom and work place). But I came to assume that spit somehow coalesces with the Chinese concept of health maintenance. If illnesses (and in earlier times, demons) are to be cast out of the body, a good spit must be an efficacious medium of egress.

The ritual purity of the act of spitting is not a complement to modern hygiene. The Beijing-based antispitting campaigns seem to acknowledge this, as do the compromise-seeking spittoons lining hospital corridors.

Seen in its cultural context, perhaps spitting is no more polluting or unsanitary or antisocial than tobacco smoking. Certainly its practitioners are as adamant as chain-smokers. In any case, ritual behavior will continue to spit in the face of rational argumentation.

A Rube Goldberg Solution

Along with bicycles and coolie-pulled carts, the other major means of moving equipment and materials through Nanning's streets are pony carts, two-wheeled conveyances by which building materials, charcoal, whitewash, and sundry other items are transported. The ponies are tough, bushy-maned little creatures of the sort I previously associated with the northern climes of the Mongols and Kazaks, but they seem very much at home in semitropical south China. Though they respond to voice commands, are often directed without reins, and even seem to sort their way through traffic while their drivers nap, there is no way to restrain them from relieving themselves in the middle of Main Street (or on your doorstep, if they happen to be delivering your kitchen charcoal at the time).

The Chinese solution to this littering problem is little bibs suspended between the front of the cart and the rear of the pony. There the pony's biodegradables collect as the cart proceeds through the city's major paved streets. Then, when the cart reaches areas of more relaxed zoning, the driver discreetly shakes out the bib and lets the chips fall where they may. It's an ingenious solution.

I imagined a similar apparatus for spitters: a little trough hung around the neck so that humans could evacuate their respiratory passages without injury or insult to passers-by.

Timbers being transported in the traditional manner

Lion Dance, New Year's celebration

Ducks getting ready for market

A vegetable vendor, Nanning free market

Television

If the "global village" ever becomes a reality, there will be a Coke machine beside every TV set. In that sense, China is part of the global village, consuming significant amounts of Coca-Cola and American TV.

The best news is that the classic Madison Avenue version of global village life is alive and well on Chinese television: the original 1970's Coke commercial in which people of all colors, creeds, and nationalities were gathered "to teach the world to sing in perfect harmony." It's the real thing, dubbed in perfect Mandarin.

America's other contributions to Chinese culture include *My Favorite Martian* (shown in China as *My Uncle Martin*) and old Disney cartoons. *Martian* was apparently a hit, having been rerun two or three times. Somehow vintage Disney cartoons of the forties, when the artwork was at its peak, have all wound up on Chinese TV. "Mandarin duck" takes on new meaning when Donald goes into a tirade. These are the great old cartoons in which Mickey, Donald, and Goofy are three pals hanging out and having adventures. (Seeing them again reminded me of the first existential question of my childhood: whether Goofy was a dog. If so, why was he Mickey's pal, while Pluto galumphed around on all fours and was only Mickey's pet? This still bothers me. In fact, I rate it as one of life's more interesting curiosities, right up there with the Shroud of Turin.) What Chinese television does very well is costume-drama miniseries. Some are rousing tales set in dynastic China with spunky, pretty young kung fu masters and women warriors battling evil landlords or tyrannical Buddhist monks.

Also popular are 1930's Shanghai gangster movies in which blue-eyed devils force pretty young rural kung fu masters and high-fashion Chinese bimbos into a life of crime. These always contain martial arts melees with hatchets as sidearms. Blood, dismembering, and disemboweling are the norm. The male lead is always lured into a life of depraved pleasure—fluid-drive DeSotos and equally speedy ladies—but regrets every fetid, funfilled moment of criminality. He finally dies with a hatchet in his back and the arch villain's intestines in his hands.

The moral, of course, is that capitalist crime doesn't pay. However, as in all first-class gangster movies and in real life, it pays very well and seems to be great fun right up to the point when your upper colon is draped over the bannister. The Chinese are playing with dynamite in trying to prove a moral lesson with this subject matter. Gangsters always wear the best suits and always will. Their girlfriends fall out of the best dresses and always will. It's all much too entertaining to be morally uplifting as well.

Running Amok

The term "amok," or "amuck," seems to have its origins in the Tagalog and Malay languages, but variations appear throughout southern Asia. Charles Allen, in *Tales from the South China Seas,* notes one definition as "self-liberation through revolt." The term also seems to have special relevance among people whose normal behavior is characterized more by passivity than by violence. I never considered any special associations among passivity, running amok, and self-liberation until I had lived in China for a year.

In the matter of passive resistance, the Chinese could have instructed Mohandas Gandhi. When they believe it will serve their purpose, the Chinese can do an incredible imitation of a rock. They will avert their eyes, assume an expression midway between saintliness and idiocy, become mute, and stand with knees bent and shoulders hunched in order to appear as small as possible—in the hope of avoiding detection altogether or, at least, being considered too insignificant for attention. If standing is not necessary, they will hunker down into a near-fetal position.

Some illustrations:

A. In the classroom, a student who deems a question (or the expectation of a response) inappropriate will suddenly become catatonic, unable to respond to or look at his tormentor. By this, I don't mean uncooperative so much as inorganic. Usually this tenacious passivity outlasted my irritation or confusion, leaving me anxious to be diverted to any other subject.

B. In Yunnan province, I witnessed a Yi woman catch up to a man she had been pursuing down the street. She yelled like a banshee (or a Yi), grabbed his wrist, and proceeded to pull him back in the direction from which they both had come. His only resistance was a mumbled protest, followed by dropping to his knees to be dragged like a child. In Sichuan province, I saw a variant of this same pattern between a peach vendor and another street shrew. In both of these instances, the passively immovable objects were met by irresistible forces.

C. On public buses already filled to the point of metal fatigue, I saw peasants hunch in the stairwell, jamming the door, in the hope that the same behavior would gain them transportation. The only response to the driver's threats and other passengers' nudges is that the trespasser's posture closes into a more complete fetal curl.

In the countryside, peasants from remote villages walk miles to a main road, then wait indefinitely at the side of the road to flag down any vehicle headed in the right direction. They are prepared to ride under any conditions and reject out-of-hand any argument about crowding. If any part of their body gains access to the vehicle they are prepared to occupy that space even if doing so immobilizes the bus or van.

In one case, it took fourteen minutes of argument that became invective, nudges that became shoves, and finally a soldier's threatening advance to evacuate a false-fetus half-lodged in the stairwell. The man then literally ran from the bus—not in fear, but in frustration, having absorbed all the humiliation and loss of face he could endure and still having failed to get the ride he desperately wanted. It was then I began to realize the near-rage that empowers the catatonia so often shown by the Chinese. They dare not express their anger for fear of it being uncontrollable to the point of running amok. When this man abandoned his immobility, he was flushed with emotion, and his body, in its jerky haste, showed signs of adrenalin overload. He had nearly lost control, and simultaneously the intended victims of his passivity were nearly aroused to violence.

Obviously this is a high-risk head game being played. Casual violence in a population so densely congested can be incredibly destructive, so any hint of physical violence is to be repressed. The passivist is attempting to achieve his goal by exploiting the cultural mandate against violence. By doing "nothing" in the face of reasoning, pleading, and even threats, he hopes to blackmail his adversary into also finally doing nothing. The real danger is that the confrontation will escalate as the anger of both parties increases. Most foreign residents who frequent marketplaces and streets away from the tourist ghettos have witnessed instances of such berserkers. In China, as elsewhere, extreme passivity can be a prelude to running amok. And there are times when an individual who runs amok seems to perceive this action as self-liberation through revolt.

D. Another case in point occurred during a sweltering morning in early June. I had become adept at ignoring extraneous noise, yet I was vaguely aware that sirens had been blaring intermittently for over an hour. A student had come by to ask me to read and edit some letters of application for study abroad. We had just finished the letters when Mary returned from class. We all had a casual conversation, then the student left. In two minutes, he returned, short of breath and greatly agitated, announcing that the university president and several other school officers had been attacked in the president's office and "disemboweled."

This was not the normal sort of campus rumor. As I was at the time headed for the post office, which took me past the president's office, I went to corroborate the disemboweling. At the intersection by the administration building, there was a crowd too dense for me to ride my bicycle through. I detoured around and continued to the post office, knowing that first more rumors and then eventually the facts would be presented one by one for me to assemble.

By the next day, I learned that "disemboweling" was an exaggeration and that no one was dead. However, it wasn't for lack of effort. A former student, wielding two butcher knives, had burst into the president's office during a meeting. In a rage, he severely wounded the president and five other office staff members before fleeing the building. He continued to run about the campus, butcher knives flashing, finally finding himself cornered on a rooftop. There, his will for suicide failed him and he docilely, passively surrendered to the certainty of Chinese justice.

Complete and final dismissal from the university is an uncommonly severe measure in this system, and for this individual would have meant returning to the grim reality of rural peasant life, as well as the accompanying loss of face for himself and his family. Apparently he had tried every ploy, including passive refusal to leave campus, to mitigate this decision. When all failed, he ran amok in the south Asian tradition. This all occurred during the month we left the university, so I was not present to see the closing events of the drama. But the responses I did witness were interesting. There was little public expression of grief for the victims— only great humiliation and fear of loss of face for the institution. The university officials with whom I dealt were almost unable to face me to receive my expressions of regret, let alone talk about it.

Slowly, an official version was put together for public consumption. Key words began to fall in place. The young man was now referred to as "not a student." This distanced him from the institution, making his actions inexplicable and therefore due to mental illness (and also serving to remove the slightest hint that this could have anything to do with student protests occurring at other universities). The word most often used to describe the event was "accident."

Changing Money

"Do you want to change?" he asked, smiling beatifically.

Was this guy rehearsing to be a TV evangelist or offering a self-help course?

"Do you want to change?" he repeated for my confused benefit.

He didn't look like Jerry Falwell or Timothy Leary. He looked like Jack Palance with jaundice, but he smiled nicely and wore a terrific leather jacket. He didn't want to improve my soul or my sensitivity, though. He wanted to make me rich.

To understand Chinese money changing, you need to know that China has two separate currency systems: *renmembi* (literally "the people's money") and Foreign Exchange Currency (F.E.C.).

Renmembi is the internal currency used by all Chinese. Its basic unit is the *yuan* (sometimes called the *yin,* and in the south frequently called the *kwai*). There are ten *jao* (or *mao*) in each yuan, and ten fen in each jao. So, you can think of fen as pennies, jao as dimes, and yuan as dollars. On international exchange, the yuan is pegged to the U.S. dollar, and for years the value has been about Y 3.60 = $1.00.

F.E.C. has the same denominations and units as renmembi, and technically one yuan of renmembi is equal to one yuan of F.E.C. Foreigners (in theory) are to spend only F.E.C. inside China; and, as the name states, they've exchanged their own foreign currency for it.

China created the two-currency system for the same reason it built the Great Wall: To keep China pure and to segregate decadent foreigners. Any item that is imported into China can only be purchased with F.E.C. This is to ensure that Chinese buy and consume Chinese products, not the products of foreign devils. This keeps the people pure and untouched by acquired foreign tastes and also does wonders for China's international balance of payments in imports-exports.

The goal is to severely limit the imports coming into the country and thus minimize Chinese money being spent outside China. F.E.C. also helps to sustain a segregated, more expensive economy for tourists by being the only currency used in the hotels, restaurants, Friendship Stores, and material oases created just for foreigners.

The hole in the Great Currency Wall is the foreign residents—teachers, businesspeople, technicians, and so forth. These foreigners live outside the oases, in conditions similar to the Chinese. Therefore, the Chinese government pays them in renmembi. But, as no renmembi is allowed to be taken out of China, the government also issues a white card (permit) for these foreigners to spend renmembi, as even a foreign devil needs to take some money home after a year or more of working in China. Those with foreign expert status (and many others as well) are allowed to exchange a percentage of their salary into F.E.C., which can be taken out of China. Thus, many resident foreigners wind up being able to spend both currencies. The black market in F.E.C. developed because many Chinese want to be able to buy foreign imports and luxury items, and those with Hong Kong connections also want to be able to send money there. So, 1.00 F.E.C. will bring anywhere from Y 1.3 to Y 1.6 renmembi, depending upon what city you're in. It is an underground economy of huge proportion.

"Do you want to change?" is the Kunming greeting to Westerners. "One hundred forty renmembi for one hundred F.E.C." Hey, everybody does it! Everybody's cheerful. A simple question, among friends, always with a smile.

Only the little herds of Sani women, who also sell their handcrafted bags, purses, and dresses, go in for the hard sell. First they hawk their handicrafts, then switch to "change money?" They hang on, hoping no will become yes. A little badgering, then a smile of resignation.

The leather-jacketed Moslem Chinese are more laid back. Their attitude is that they're offering a good product and they know it, and the Wall Street of the Kunming currency market is upstairs over the coffee shop. Not *which* coffee shop, the *only* coffee shop—at least the only one I ever found in a city where some shops are so small you can pass two of them in one stride.

The place is narrower than a Toyota van. You buy a ticket up front and walk sideways past the standard Chinese restaurant tables and stools (like the play desk and chairs you had as a kid) to the back, where the steam-drenched kitchen is. Then you wave your ticket at four or five kitchen workers who ignore you for several minutes.

The victimized worker who is compelled to wait on a foreign devil takes your ticket and shuffles over to a seething cauldron, where he dips into an ebony liquid and pours it into a handle-less mug.

"Sugar?"

"Yes, please! Sugar!" Anything to dilute the caffeine-laden venom called Yunnan coffee (a local product, hardly exported—for the same reason you can't carry guns on airplanes). But you'll need it for what lies ahead—or, more precisely, overhead. You are going upstairs, to the inner temple of the money changers.

The staircase, designed by M.C. Esher, appears to lead directly into a wall: it's so narrow that only from what looks like the top step can you see another flight at a right angle to the first. After this turn, there is no going back. The mug burns your hand, but it's the other palm that's sweaty. Once upstairs, Cheshire-cat smiles mark your path like Burma Shave signs. Here nobody asks, "Do you want to change money?" It's, "Do you have F.E.C. or Hong Kong?" "How much?" "From where have you come?" "What's the rate there?" "Would you like to take a little something to Hong Kong?" All with a smile—so many smiles, you begin to think you're in a very weird Coca-Cola commercial.

A venerable old gentleman handled my account. He had a Texas Instruments calculator, refined speech, and better English than my students. Throughout our chat, he addressed me as "Sir."

On the other hand, Maxwell, a five-year veteran of teaching in Beijing, was a nice man, too, but with just the hint of the inside dopester about him. He enjoyed the storehouse of information he had acquired through seniority, and the special *cachet* this gave him with recently arrived foreign faculty. "Just last week, two foreign experts were given 24 hours to leave the country or a Chinese prison stay!" he had announced in response to a query about the exchange rate on the "black" in Beijing. I hadn't doubted Maxwell's sincerity. His point was that doing black market currency just then was probably difficult and definitely dangerous.

(I did have some doubts about the story, as it was based on a report in *China Daily,* which is used regularly to tell foreigners what Chinese want foreigners to know. That's why discerning foreigners read it: to see what you should publicly believe. And to read sporadic U.S. sports stories on the international sports page—though it made me crazy that they printed the baseball box scores but not the league standings.)

What is to be concluded? In Kunming, Dali, Guanzhou, Shanghai, Guilin, Chengdu, even Lhasa, money changers are ubiquitous. They are all aware of the exchange rates in other cities. A German student from Shanghai told me of trading money in broad daylight on the steps of the Bank of China a few feet from a police officer. He told me he wouldn't have done it if it hadn't been his regular dealer, and that the dealer was indifferent to the presence of the police.

Everywhere, money changing is illegal. Everywhere the dealers are outrageously blatant about their business, even in Beijing, the center of government and of party authority. A cynic might think someone in a government position of great authority is allowing all this to happen. That would be one way to ensure that lots of F.E.C. would wind up in government hands and not in private hands.

Anyway, all of this should be publicized, like the warning on cigarette labels:

Warning! Black market currency exchanging is hazardous to your status as a gracious guest of China. It is illegal, immoral, and antisocialist. It is decadent, bourgeois profiteering. Once begun, it is addictive and can have long-term effects upon your financial status.

FIVE

✧ ✧ ✧ ✧ ✧ ✧ ✧

Excursions

To Rongxian

When we passed the brick foundry, Professor Wang raised both his hands, smiled, and explained through translation that he had spent the Cultural Revolution doing manual labor at a similar brickworks. That was his "reeducation" after he had been "struggled against."

Being struggled against is bitter, black humor. During the Cultural Revolution, it meant having teenage banshees enter your home, destroy anything modern, functional, and attractive for being bourgeois, then being publicly abused, psychologically and/or physically. If you were good at "self-criticism," then perhaps you could be successfully reeducated through menial labor (Chairman Deng had been a janitor).

What started in Wang's throat as a cynic's chuckle quickly degenerated into a chain-smoker's hack. Professor Wang was abstaining from smoking in the van for the collective welfare of us seven other passengers. He was nobly and rather obviously sacrificing one of life's pleasures for our sakes—this, from a man whose banquet behavior was to eat the odd peanut or the cold dumpling because the main course of life should be conversation, tumblers of rice wine, and cigarettes. About every hour and a half, he announced that the rest of us needed to stretch our legs. As we stretched, he smoked two Mango-brand cigarettes.

The Toyota van was full to the brim with eight passengers (five Chinese, three foreign guests). This meant at least three simultaneous and continuous conversations, one or more always taking the tortuous track of translation. The cassette music was played at such a high volume I expected to see stress lines of metal fatigue appear in the van's body, but this was a level the Chinese consider cheerful. We had started the trip with very perky Chinese versions of Muzak that included, typically, lots of Stephen Foster ("My Old Kentucky Home" was given a full orchestral treatment; and "Oh, Susanna," a great favorite in China, was sung by a flood of voices). When that tape was followed by Hong Kong disco, it was more than a man without cigarettes could endure. Above all the other sounds, Wang barked at Meng, who was acting as DJ, and the tape was changed. At the same volume, on came Beethoven's Fifth Symphony, Wang's own favorite. He smiled benignly, which, with his nicotine-stained teeth, was somehow menacing.

We proceeded down the road. We also proceeded in spite of the road and, sometimes, in the absence of the road. As the trip unfolded, the pavement changed from smooth to crater-pocked. The craters disappeared where the pavement ended and the excavation for anticipated pavement began. Excavated roadbed turned into dirt track, and as rain began to fall, this turned into buffalo wallow—sometimes shared with just such creatures, as well as bicyclists, pedestrians, three-wheeled tractor-trucks, three-wheeled taxis, and suicidal motorcyclists. On this journey to the city of Rongxian, we saw the aftermaths of six wrecks. On the way home, we would see two more.

My fellow travelers had come prepared not only with good music, but also lots of snacks. Among other treats, we had bags of rice wafers, sunflower seeds, fruit, water-buffalo jerky with a tangy sauce dried into it, and something like the stones or pits from fruit that had been soaked in strange flavors to be sucked like gumballs. In spite of this bounty, we stopped for lunch—though it took the driver a full hour to find a roadside restaurant he thought appropriate for foreigners. ("Too many flies," he would report back and continue the search fifty yards down the road.) When at last he gave his seal of approval, we were in a closed area of the province where foreigners went only by special dispensation. It was like when Clint Eastwood enters the saloon: all eyes were on the door. By now, however, we were used to it. We were directed to the biggest table, near the open kitchen, where we could select our food and watch it being cooked.

I left food selection to the others and followed hand directions to the "restroom"—through an open courtyard, past a pigsty, to a sheltered trough slanted away from the restaurant. In a basket cage next to the trough, a solitary chicken awaited its fate, stoically blinking through the rain and the splash I unintentionally contributed. Later, as we ate, the same bird was brought into the kitchen and very professionally dispatched.

After lunch, we continued our journey, which in a sense had begun about three weeks prior in the sitting room of Professor Wang's apartment. Wang was a professor in the philosophy department at the university. This meant he taught modern philosophy with a heavy injection of Marxist dialectical imperative. However, as "history of philosophy," he could indulge his passion for Taoism.

He spoke no English (and I spoke moron Chinese), but his desire to communicate overcame this barrier. Conroy served as our interpreter. Our discussions began respectfully and carefully, as we each asked questions about ideas and writers of our common knowledge. But slowly Wang's enthusiasm and opinions took charge. A natural mime, he would start an animated monologue, gesticulating and lecturing. He would produce chalk from the pocket of his Mao jacket (he seemed to always have chalk in his pocket, just in case), drop to his knees, and begin writing and drawing on the cement floor of the apartment. In the next room his wife would sigh, cast an indulgent glance at her fevered husband and his weirdly supportive foreign guests, move to the kitchen, and produce covered mugs of soothing chrysanthemum tea.

At my initial meeting with Wang, I had expressed my own interest in the common ground between early science and traditional lore. Inadvertently, I had rung the right chime. (The reason the English scholar Joseph Needham is so revered in China is his focus on the scientific aspects of traditional Chinese culture.) At a subsequent meeting, in one of those coincidences that permeate a foreigner's life in China, we were joined by Meng.

Slowly, coyly, tantalizingly, like the lifting of Salome's veils, it was revealed that Meng was a construction engineer, that he and Wang were collaborating on a paper, and that the paper focused on an old Taoist pavilion. They had a manuscript in progress, complete with architectural drawings and construction details. An element of Taoist philosophy is the idea that the spiritual is best revealed to the consciousness through physical applications. A unique design element of the pavilion is that the interior pillars are suspended a fraction of an inch short of the floor. Thus, the structure can safely shift with any seismic tremor. To Meng and Wang this was evidence of the incorporation of Taoist philosophy into the building design, an illustration of the yin-yang, flexibility-rigidity concept. There followed a spasm of chalk talk on the floor.

As Wang lectured, his cat wandered into the room and sat on the chalked yin-yang. At that propitious moment, Wang announced that we should all make a pilgrimage to view and meditate on this architectural wonder. All the travel details would be arranged for me and I should be prepared to leave sometime in the next month. As I was not asked whether this fit my plans, I was left to wonder how he had trained the cat to sit on the yin-yang.

From that auspicious beginning, the jaunt to Rongxian was born. (Rongxian, a day's travel from Nanning, is the government center of Rongxian County, still in Guangxi Province but near the border of Guangdong Province.) We were driven to the government guesthouse, which had just opened the previous year. Already it had taken on the ramshackle appearance that is the fate of all Chinese accommodations. But the greeting was effusive: there were more people to help with luggage than there were pieces of luggage.

We were escorted to a meeting room furnished in the regulation manner: a fixed square of tall-backed, wooden armchairs surrounding a square of low coffee tables. The chairs all had antimacassars. The tables were laden with covered tea mugs, packs of cigarettes (Wang opened the first pack, beaming like an orphan at his first Christmas party), and bowls of strange fruit. The fruit was introduced even before some of the lesser officials. We Westerners call them palmelos. They are like archaic grapefruit, a product of the Rongxian region and a point of pride. They would appear at every teatime and at most meals, and we were given boxes full at our departure. Fortunately, they were delicious.

Told to refresh ourselves, we were seated in one line of the tall chairs. Our hosts sat facing us, "reading our papers," as we sipped tea and devoured palmelos. Of course they had been in possession of our papers for a week and had already studied them privately, but protocol had to be followed. The papers detailed that we were honored guests, that we had come to admire and meditate on the Ming dynasty Taoist pavilion that crowns the hillside above the river, and that if duly impressed we might add our names to a roster urging that the site be designated as a National Heritage, which would ensure its preservation and bring distinction to the locality. The papers went on to indicate that, in the interest of friendship, we three foreigners would all give speeches to the students and staff of Rongxian Middle School. After a ritual of decision making, it was announced that we were excellent and welcome guests and that we were invited to a banquet in thirty minutes. We all looked relieved and surprised.

Like so many of China's treasures, the pavilion was in the middle of a well-worn residential/commercial area concealed behind a brick wall and an iron gate. Once through the gate, you entered a different environment. The entryway wound along an incline of flagstone steps up the riverbank. At the top of the stairs, through an archway, at the end of about fifty yards of paving stone, sat the object of our pilgrimage. At the arch, the pavilion (not a true temple, as it was never inhabited by monks) was a three-story wedding cake of elaborate tiled roofs densely populated with creatures both real and mythical. Seagoing and earth-slithering reptiles seemed to nearly slip off the edges. A blazing sphere topped by a calabash was at the very top.

At close proximity, after crossing the fifty-yard approach, the dominant impression was massive structure of dark wood. The local tung oil is a clear wood preservative having only residual color, but when applied for centuries, in this case perhaps seven of them, it collects to a brown-black tone. The structure was built, and sustains its structural integrity, without nails. There are only bamboo pegs in the roof frames, over which tiles are laid. The corner posts and interior columns are massive tree trunks stripped of limbs and bark, cut from their roots but seemingly reincarnated as living supports of a building designed to move and sigh with the earth. The notches for the post and lintel construction were cut with a tolerance such that the building can shift but not lean under stresses.

In this construction, the philosopher and the engineer demonstrated the practicality, even the rationality, of Taoism. The foci of their premise are the interior beams, which extend the full heights of the top two stories of the pavilion. Each is a massive, continuous tree trunk extending from the ceiling of the third level to nearly the floor of the second level. Thus they are suspended from the ceiling, nearly but never quite touching the floor. Like a self-supporting arch, the suspended interior weight draws the building in on itself, gaining solidity from flexibility.

Duly impressed, I tried to shake its beauty from my eyes and see it only as a building puzzle. But of course it was puzzling only because of its beauty—a good lesson in aesthetics.

Rain had fallen the entire morning and the wet was seeping into our bones. Eventually we were directed to a work shed overlooking the river. Here we warmed our hands on tea mugs and acknowledged the chill we had previously ignored. Now we were asked to express our reactions in "the book." Just a few words, perhaps a poem, even a sketch, our feelings—a small request. But the book turned out to be large sheets of rice paper, measuring about two by three feet. We were supplied with an inkstone and brushes and we each in turn stood over a desk with the rice paper, weighted at each corner, laid before us. For Meng and Wang, who wrote in the traditional running script, which flows down the length of the page, the paper was pulled slowly away as they drew their calligraphic characters, their hands moving only at the wrist. I became more clumsy of hand and mind when I realized the nature of the book: each page, assigned to one person, would be bound to the others for special display; our words and penmanship would join the pavilion in its procession through the ages. Whatever I wrote may now be immortal but was certainly not memorable.

This process went on for nearly two hours. It was given full attention by, and seemed to render total pleasure to, all my Chinese companions. Each sheet was watched intently as the writer-artist left his best effect. It continued to be admired as it was laid carefully to dry. There was a raptness to their involvement, like the concentration children can give to their fantasy play or craftsmen bring to their creative process. Of my months among my Chinese friends, I now look back on these hours as the time when they were at their most "Chinese": absorbed in a process of potent cultural meaning to them and (for once) oblivious to my foreignness. As my page dried, my companions stared at it intently, conferred in hushed tones, and settled on a translation, which was then inscribed in the corner; undoubtedly a generous civilizing of the original.

The next morning we were summoned to breakfast by the usual discreet knock on the door. But this morning we were told to "prepare ourselves psychologically." As it had stopped raining, we were to give our speeches outside on the playing field of Rongxian Middle School. This meant that we would address all 1,000 students instead of the 300 that would have been compressed into a meeting room, so we should prepare ourselves. For me, this consisted of eating several extra steamed dumplings for breakfast.

When we arrived at the gate of the school, the driveway was already lined with adolescents. The entire student body was standing in the mist, looking avid, certain that this was a great event, or at least a nice break in the routine. They beamed, giggled, nudged one another, and shifted position as though certain that they could, by trial and error, find an appropriate appearance. I was equally in the dark about what conduct was called for by the situation, but there's no way to outwiggle or outstare a thousand adolescents. Our escort indicated that we were going to walk up the driveway past the teen throng and that I would lead the way.

From TV coverage of U.S. political campaigns, I know about working the crowd. So I fantasized that I was running for alderman with the full backing of the "machine." I nodded, spoke greetings to no one in particular, made eye contact, and kept moving. Like a member of the politburo, I applauded the applause. They applauded me applauding the applause. Everyone in our group went through the same little choreography as they walked the gauntlet. We arrived at the crest of the driveway and walked into the ramshackle compound that typifies Chinese schoolyards. We were ushered into a small meeting room, the usual chairs surrounding a square of tables, covered tea mugs, and our old friends, the palmelos. We were to meet the school leadership, refresh ourselves, gather our wits, and go knock 'em dead.

My own wit was wandering to thoughts about adolescent energy and the manner in which it was marshalled to state purpose in China. Walking up that driveway, I had had a moment of terror. As I felt all that positive energy beaming at me, and I had fantasized back fifteen years, when a similar age group and its energy were harnessed to the tyranny of the Cultural Revolution. The same unquestioning devotion to purpose had propelled adolescent groups on search-and-destroy missions during which they vandalized, humiliated, and maimed their teachers and elders. What if, halfway up the drive, someone in Beijing had thrown the switch from positive to negative?

The same sea of bright faces was now massed on the playing field. Those in front were seated on the tiny chairs and stools seen everywhere in China. They whispered and wiggled with great expectations. It was like the moment of contact in the film *Close Encounters of the Third Kind*. We were the local version of the little embryonic space travelers who finally toddle out of the mother ship. Our kind had not passed through here before. Literally, for most of those students, we were the first Westerners and the first native English speakers they had ever encountered. The actual message of communication here, as in the movie, was not as significant as the contact itself. Slowly, I spoke to them on the topic assigned to me by our hosts, "Chinese-American

Friendship." Comprehension of the platitudes registered on some faces; others were tuned to their own muse. In turn, we each did our best at cultural exchange. After the speeches, we exchanged small gifts and clichés with the school's president and the local party chairman.

This was the point at which rock stars are spirited away by limousine. Not that well equipped, we began to walk away like normal people, forgetting our celebrity status and the price of fame. Immediately, each of us was surrounded by little herds of autograph seekers. Individually they were polite, but the collective press of their bodies was like a rugby scrum. They compacted around me until I couldn't keep my pen in contact with the paper. Ultimately the shouts of school officers diluted the mobs and we walked away unscathed. I hope Andy Warhol was right, because fifteen minutes of fame was quite enough for me. Back at the meeting room, the faculty were much more restrained. They were, in fact, almost silent. One young teacher, designated or self-appointed, initiated most of the faculty's comments. This was the English-teaching faculty. Some spoke very little of their subject language. We talked to the young teacher and a few others who became emboldened enough to ask questions. It turned out that at least three had studied Russian for most of their college years; then one day, when the political winds shifted, they were told they were English teachers. So much for career planning in China.

Whether out of respect, timidity, indifference, or even resentment, the discussion was uneasy. The teachers are required to spend ten hours per day with their students. We had just spent two hours and received more praise than they will get in their lives. Worse, in fifteen minutes we could leave for good. Conceivably, they could spend their entire lives working in these shabby, ill-equipped classrooms. What could we say to them to make it better? Only thank you.

Three Graces taking the evening sun, Rongxian

Students at Rongxian Middle School

A meat vendor, marketplace north of Dali

Fish traps drying at Lake Erhai, north of Dali

It was time to leave. We were driven back to the guesthouse for a final banquet and to stuff our bags into the van. The trip had gone well for both hosts and guests. Everyone had behaved appropriately and done what they were supposed to do. Now I had the sense that we were all anxious to terminate it before anyone messed up. So we shared our last feast, dredging up any remaining unused compliments, posed for the required group pictures, and waved good-bye. It all felt good except for the precognition of the eight hours of bad road, perky music, and cigarette rationing that stretched ahead.

To Dali and Beyond

When it appears on maps of Yunnan province, it is variously spelled Tali or Dali. Either way, it has long been the rest stop for traders and travelers entering or exiting China from the west. Marco Polo was only one such visitor. He described thriving marketplaces and vigorous people with eyes and hair coloring that suggested genes were being traded as well.

Veterans of the Asian travel circuit compare Dali to other countries (Nepal, mainly) rather than to other places in China. It has become the favorite Chinese watering hole for the New Age hippie-types who still migrate through India, trek in northern Thailand, and risk intestinal seizures from the tacos and pizza in Kathmandu. (Actually there are two types of New Age hippie: one is the backpacking, under-thirty student doing a last trek before settling into paying taxes. These migrate in multinational coed flocks from point to point, and disband and regroup at various places in the Asian circuit. The other variety, equally numerous, is the front-loaded, hot-water-seeking, over-thirty teacher-consultant who stoically rides the same buses and flocks in smaller, more permanent bands. Most are teachers; some are technical consultants. A surprising number of them travel with children.)

Dali can be reached only by foot or by bus. From Kunming, it is a ten-hour bus ride; the highway follows much of the old Burma Road "over the hump," past rice-paddy-terraced mountains and switchbacks along mountain streams. It seems like one long, beautiful curve constantly bending back on itself as it rises to the sky. We were sitting in the back row of the bus munching sesame cookies, enjoying the scenic beauty and the bus's loopy assault on the angled road, when a young Chinese male stood up on his seat to hang the upper third of his body out the window and, with the wind's help, sprayed the side of the bus with his morning congee. This performance was repeated by other Chinese with a regularity that gave explicit meaning to the term, "ad nauseum."

In Dali, all foreigners are delivered to the Number Two Hotel—the only hotel for foreigners. The Number One is twenty kilometers away in Xiaguan. Tour groups are delivered to the Number One, then bussed to Dali for day trips. The relative quality of hotels is what separates the tourists from the travelers. The Number Two has nice ambience but horrific plumbing. Although there are enough rooms (or, more accurately, cubicles) for up to 300 guests, there are only two toilets, one for each sex. For days at a time, there will be no water for flushing. The measure of Dali's charm was such that a determined core of Westerners stayed on through the worst of these plumbing malfunctions— when the toilets were without water and the first-floor hallway was flooded by a broken pipe.

In spite of the Amityville plumbing, the hotel was a mellow scene. In the mornings, a half-speed wake-up game of volleyball evolved among Chinese locals and varieties of foreigners. Then people strolled around the stands of the adjoining playing field, seeking the sun, schmoozing, and exchanging travel tips, experiences, and exaggerations. The temperature is never much above sixty degrees, but the sunshine at 7,000 feet is still therapeutic, especially for the Beijing refugees.

Dali is an irresistible combination of Eastern weirdness and Western breakfasts. Across town, one of the three pagodas has leaned like the Tower of Pisa since the 1925 earthquake. During the same earthquake, a great bronze garuda (which to my heathen eyes looks like a big chicken) fell from this pagoda top along with a bronze globe that split open, revealing a manuscript. The resident ruling official took a look at this ancient treasure and promptly distributed it, page by page, to his political cronies. Just around the corner from the hotel is the public bathhouse, everyone's sanctuary from bad plumbing. Here, attendants lead you to marble tubs and, after a hot soak, massage your cares away. At the hotel they serve coffee in glasses, barley flour pancakes, and pagoda burgers. Across town, barley-flour pizza is served with chopsticks at the Coco-Cola Restaurant.

If you want to shop your cares away, Monday is the day to do it. Centuries ago, Marco Polo described the market fairs of the area, and fifty years ago, J.F.C. Rock described the market north of Dali and the hordes of Min Chia (now called Bai), Yi, and Na-Khi who frequented it. What is certainly the same market continues each Monday, organized by the collective unconscious of the ethnic minorities of Yunnan. Unchanged is the array of jewelry, beads, amber, trinkets, embroidery, brass locks, ritual paraphernalia, beeswax, various slaughtered animals, breads, spices, ceremonial knives, funeral shoes, baby carriers, firewood, and livestock—except for the three-wheeled tractors that lunge through the crowd belching noise and black smoke.

More threatening than the tractors are the Bai and Yi women: they command the right-of-way, dare you to bargain, and wait for no man to be served before themselves. Rock described their female ancestors doing most of the labor, handling the finances, and periodically accosting the occasional male met on the trail. Voracious converts to the Communist Revolution in the late

1930s, they drilled and marched to the tune of "John Brown's body lies a-Moldering in the grave." Rock offered no explanation for this. (Perhaps Agnes Smedley struck again.)

Raiders of the Lost Flashlight

The Na-Khi shepherd girls sang Chinese songs learned in school and performed little choreographed disco steps they learned from TV. In turn, Conroy and I gave a mournful rendition of "Home on the Range"—the state song of Kansas but equally appropriate to the 9000-foot plain near the base of Jade Dragon Mountain. Even the sheer joy of hearing such a manly air did not weaken their resolve to sing none of their native Na-Khi songs. Well might you ask how it came to pass that we should be trading melodies with young shepherd girls in the mountains of Yunnan Province.

It all started with a quest—for the flashlight of J.F.C. Rock. As you will recall, recent rumor had placed it in Lijiang, the ancient capital of Yunnan, the center of the even more ancient Na-Khi culture; and for more than twelve years the base of operations for one of life's more productive misfits, Joseph Francis Charles Rock.

Quite by serendipity, and at a time when I was searching for a project that would divert my thoughts from my palsied face and Lon Chaney smile, I heard of an American botanist-ethnographer who had wandered around Yunnan Province in the 1920s and 1930s. J.F.C. Rock: the name alone had an irresistible resonance. If that hadn't been his name, he would have invented something equally romantic. In a sense, he is one of those characters who invented himself. Born in Austria to a guilt-immersed Lutheran family, he fled that existence by taking ship after ship around the world, finally coming to rest in Hawaii in 1907. Along the way, he acquired languages as casually as others catch colds, became an expert on tropical botany, and was so duly impressed by these abilities that he conferred a Ph.D. upon himself.

His actual skills were such that early in his career no one questioned his academic credentials, and when he died at age seventy-nine in 1962, his accomplishments were so impressive that no one cared. Through expeditions and publications he had become an authority on lobelias, rhododendrons, blight-resistant chestnuts, and most of the flora of Hawaii, Burma, and southwest China.

It was on such a botanical expedition that he first came to the mountain areas of Yunnan and settled near Lijiang in the early 1930s, living there in virtual isolation from the modern world until forced to flee the Japanese during World War II. In Lijiang, his attention was divided between the botany and an equally endangered species, the Na-Khi.

He never really explained his fascination with the Na-Khi; he simply devoted the better part of twenty years to documenting their traditional life-style and religion. It isn't even clear whether he liked them, but he spent the most productive years of his life with them, became the foremost authority on their dying traditional culture, and in doing so left one of the few accurate portrayals of life in China's western provinces before World War II. The fact that he valued the ethnic cultures of China before the Han Chinese did, is enough to offend the Chinese academic establishment. So today, in China, his efforts are grudgingly acknowledged by Chinese scholars.

One of Rock's major achievements was to compile a dictionary of the Na-Khi syllabic language and an inventory of the Na-Khi pictographic language. The syllabic language is the older of the two, having its roots in Tibet. The pictographic language was devised by Na-Khi shamans to keep their rites and ceremonies secret from commoners. The pictograms were learned by memory and had several layers of cryptic meaning. Even in Rock's time, the real meanings of both languages were being lost. Rock worked feverishly with the remaining elder shamans, trying to secure proper translations before it was too late. (Yet a young Chinese scholar in Kunming blithely told me his coworkers are now, nearly fifty years later, doing the correct systematic translations with contemporary Na-Khi informants. So it goes.)

At any rate, Lijiang in northern Yunnan had been opened to foreigners in 1986. From Nanning it was only a plane ride to Kunming, from Kunming only a day's bus ride to Dali, and from Dali only one more day on the bus to Lijiang. To whet my appetite, Conroy whispered to me a secondhand rumor that someone had actually seen Rock's flashlight. It would have been churlish to question him closely on the pedigree of such freely given inside information.

Abandoning the ample pleasures of Dali's mountain-high living, we had come to the base of Jade Dragon Mountain, to the old section of Lijiang where canals run in front of the shops and domiciles, where old Na-Khi women embroider star-shaped discs with which they decorate the backs of their cloaks to indicate that they work even at night. (Unfortunately, they work so much they haven't refined their cooking much past burning things on a wood fire. Restaurants there are medieval canteens: our first Lijiang breakfast consisted of fried barley cakes over which were spread sugar and animal fat—a rib-sticking dish, if it ever moves that far along the digestive tract. This was served with a bowl of sweet soy milk, delightfully accented by little bits of hot pepper left in the unwashed bowl from last evening's dinner.)

So, well nourished, we began our search. As luck would have it, the stumble from the dark recesses of this gourmet establishment led to a chance encounter with a small man who looked more preserved than alive. Slowly, like a tractor starting on a cold morning, he dredged up from memory his proficient English, untapped for years. Like a singing computer, he began speaking English—with an Austrian accent: "Yah!" (J.F.C. Rock, Vienna born, had taught him the language.) I was sorely tempted to add the same accent to my Chin-glish, and could just restrain myself from heel clicking.

From him we got directions to the Dongbwa Institute, which had been established with the government's approval to house the fragments of Rock's library and collections left by him in Lijiang. We said, *"Zai gin und auf Wiedersehen,"* and set out. At the institute, I expected to encounter some wizened, venerable old sage sitting cross-legged, focusing one eye on each of us and awaiting a propitious sign. Instead, we were greeted with, "Hey, where y'all from?" A University of Chicago graduate student from Memphis was studying Na-Khi culture for his dissertation. He spoke impeccable Chinese and 'peccable Na-Khi. He had been there off and on since 1984, and continuously for the previous year. The authorities allowed him to see one manuscript at a time and hardly any of the artifacts. I immediately realized life was too short for me to make any headway via the Dongbwa Institute, although they did offer us tea. The graduate student had not heard of the flashlight but had picked up rumors of a pistol-butted shotgun used by Rock (for what? I wondered). It was rumored still to be in the village where Rock had last lived, outside Lijiang. I began to get the sense that I was living out one of those Saturday movie serials from my childhood.

But those serials were fun! And the village was only about twenty kilometers away, on a dirt track angling up to the foot of Jade Dragon Mountain. So we rented bicycles. Thirteen kilometers later, the Jade Dragon still taunted us like a mirage: always in sight, never realized. A fifteen-mile-per-hour crosswind, and perhaps a hint of age and poor physical condition, slowed our pace.

Then the shepherd girls, like sirens, had beckoned us from the path of our quest. Perhaps they knew a shortcut! Perhaps they had a six-pack! We dismounted our rented steeds and strode toward them. They were both Na-Khi, both under twelve, tending goats. One had an incipient case of pyorrhea; both had chronic cases of the giggles. They were adamant that we should proceed no further toward our goal in the mountains. Ghosts and wolves resided there. Much better that we should stay with them and sing songs. A third of the way through the Yunnan Top Forty, my attention strayed back to Jade Dragon Mountain and the lowering sun.

All was lost. We had failed to obtain the flashlight-shotgun. Like Quixote, all we could claim were inflated lyrics to "an impossible dream." We tired of Asian disco, waved *zai gin* and good-bye. Now all we had ahead of us was thirteen kilometers of bad road. Fifty yards into our return journey, we were engulfed by dust. As it cleared, we saw a stake-bed truck waiting for our company. There were two men in the cab, and six men, one woman, a dog, and a half-load of logs in the back—by local standards, it was virtually empty! Our bikes were hoisted on board, then us. Immediately the truck struggled to cruising speed. For just such an occasion, I had purchased with precious foreign exchange a pack of Asia's cigarette of preference—Marlboros. In the Chinese ritual of camaraderie, I offered cigarettes to all. In proper Chinese protocol, they refused twice and happily accepted on the third offer (all except the woman and the dog). I had forgotten matches, but it was too windy anyway. An already-lit Chinese cigarette sufficed.

I lay back to take pleasure in life: good companions who spoke not a word of any language during the entire ride, a good smoke, and a good chance at a ruptured spleen as I ricocheted from log to log—a man at peace with the world, even as my dream of the fabled flashlight-shotgun receded in the dust. As they say on TV, it just didn't get much better than this—except that the lingering Bell's palsy left my lips unable to inhale or puff on the cigarette.

I stared at the Marlboro, diminishing by its own fire. Was it just the wind and falling temperature, or a sense of mortality that sent a chill through me?

SIX

✧ ✧ ✧ ✧ ✧ ✧ ✧

Pride and Prejudice

The Blind Palmist

In any prolonged travel there is a point at which you realize that what had been exotic has become mundane. You are becoming inured to the sights, sounds, and smells that had previously enchanted your senses. I began to feel this way about Nanning's street scenes after about eight months.

When shopping downtown, I walked or pedaled as fast as possible through the same congestion of humanity I had earlier experienced as entertainment. I began to avoid the sections of the free market that displayed the snakes to be skinned while you waited, the live turtles whose next swim would be in the soup pot, the pelts of endangered species, the monkey skeletons, the tusks of unknown origin, and the roots for all occasions. For me, a Hershey bar would have been the pearl of greater price. Even the street performer with the trained snake that traveled up one nostril and out the other, or from nasal passage to mouth, couldn't hold my interest. "When the snake can do ear to ear, let me know," I thought to myself.

Then I saw the blind palmist. Actually, I had been bicycling past her for weeks before I realized exactly what she was doing. It had been hard to figure out because she was either sitting placidly on one of the tiny stools favored by street vendors, or she was surrounded by a crowd. Since it's pretty easy to draw a crowd in China, I hadn't paid much attention. She was always near the train station, where people in transit with some idle time and pocket money were a major part of the traffic.

What I noticed first was that she was fat; that's unusual enough in China, especially among southern Chinese, who are generally a small, lithe people. So here was a tallish, 200-pound woman hunkered down on a child-size stool. After riding past her several more times I observed that she apparently was blind, that she was even more interesting to the Chinese passers-by than to me, and that very often she was holding someone's hand.

Finally I added it all up and I almost fell off my bike: she was a fortune-teller, a blind palmist! In the land of Marxist scientific rationalism, she was not being hassled by the police and had her clients queuing up to hear their future. Palmistry under the best conditions is hardly an empirical process, but what does a blind palmist interpret ("Sir, either you have a very strong lifeline or a rice noodle in your hand")? How does she do it? Are there Braille points on palms that only she can perceive? All my attention, and my skepticism, was diverted to the matter of her method: how can a blind woman read a palm? What does she "see"?

Hours later, after pedaling home, I realized all my questions were focused on the most apparent, not the most relevant, issue. (When confronted with a blind palmist, I was so intrigued with how she did it, I was overlooking that what she was doing was wholly spurious or at least highly suspect.) At that moment, the blind palmist became my metaphor for China: both China and the palmist are masters at misdirecting our attention, leading us to focus on the wrong questions.

Skilled professional skeptics, political and academic, come to China to assess its future. While trying to assess the inevitable consequences of deforestation, exhausted soil, polluted water, and over a billion people (half of whom are under age twenty-five), they become mesmerized by the valid but only tangentially relevant "great strides since liberation." It's so easy, and so encouraged by the Chinese, to see only what has been achieved in the past, that hardly any observer can keep in mind the enormity of what is to come.

Just recently, I read a review of a newly published book on Chinese agriculture by a U.S. "expert" who concluded China could now grow enough food for all its people. He came to this conclusion after several months of firsthand observation, during which his Chinese hosts had escorted him from one farm site to another—each, surprise of surprises, bountifully productive.

There is no denying Chinese agricultural production has improved terrifically over the last twenty years. What his attention was diverted away from was the absence of a nationwide food storage and distribution system that could alleviate the continuous local and regional shortages. There is neither a road nor a rail system that efficiently links the disparate sectors of this huge country; and even if there were, regional rivalries are still strong enough to impede national food distribution. As with the palmist, so with every issue—population control, food production, manufacturing. It's so easy to be impressed by what's happening, you lose sight of more basic questions.

The Great Wall is a more innocuous example. It is, after all, a heck of a wall. We have to acknowledge it's awesome, and it is the only manmade object visible from the moon. It is a wonder of the world. Of course, it's also an awesome monument to human folly—a huge, immobile, defense system obsolete at conception, never completed, and vulnerable as soon as a treasonous commander was put in charge. It has been functional only in mesmerizing its own culture and, centuries later, in luring tourists into buying T-shirts. But while you are walking the Great Wall, huffing up its angularity, bracing against the frigid wind howling down from Mongolia, you cannot fail to be awed. Just as you can't fail to be impressed by a blind palmist.

Coming to Terms

Almost every foreigner in China at some point harbors the fantasy of writing a penetrating, serious book that will reveal the heart of China to the mind of the West. Something about China on the "brink of modernization," or the increase in rice production, or the new economic policy, would do nicely—something like all those penetrating, serious books you read before you came to China in order to prepare yourself for the experience. Then you realize that all those serious books left you wholly unprepared for the real thing, and the fantasy fades. There is even an oft-repeated cliché among resident foreigners: stay two weeks, write a book; two months, write an article; two years, write nothing. Part of the problem is if you stay long enough and you do not become an ideologue, then you are sure to have experiences that will contradict whatever premise and conclusion you labored over the previous six months.

Still, I felt that by now I should have some profound summary of China, the Third World, "civilization as we know it," etc. At most I can offer only one significant observation: character (personality?) is stronger than culture, and culture is stronger than ideology.

By this, I mean I am still who I am, there in China or back home. My relationships, work habits, interests, viewpoint, and their expression remain the symptoms or observable features of some psychological core that I suppose is my character. If by age forty we all have the faces we deserve, so also must we have the characters we create and preserve by our daily actions. Worse news yet, the things that worked for me at home were also efficacious there, contrary to all the cultural relativism I read and internalized. Also, in China as in my own culture there is the same spectrum of human dignity and folly.

Culture remains the context to which any viable ideology must adapt. The most thoughtful scholars on modern China (such as Richard Solomon and Sun Longji) acknowledge that Chinese Communism is more Chinese than Marxist or even Maoist. The "deep structure" (Sun Longji's term) of Confucian-based, family-centered authoritarianism is the living root and solid trunk onto which Communism has been grafted. The Manchu dynasty has been replaced by the Communist party dynasty. As Chinese culture absorbed all its conquerors, so it absorbed all its saviors and reformers and revolutionaries. As it out-endured invaders, it will out-endure ideologies.

The Ethic of Mediocrity

On December 4, 1986, the *China Daily* headline was, "Don't worry, get rich, Bo assures businesses." Bo Yibo was then the vice-chairman of the party's Central Advisory Committee and the event was the First National Meeting of Model Self-Employed Workers. As the self-employed do not have the favored status of the state-employed in China, it was rather daring to even think of them as "models" for young Chinese to emulate. But the vice-chairman did just that, saying, "Prospering private traders or workers are regarded today not as 'bourgeoisie' but as 'models' of the Chinese people." He was further quoted making the startling announcement, "Someone has to get rich ahead of the others so that the whole nation will prosper in the end."

Within weeks, official rhetoric of this tone was silenced as student demonstrators began to take it seriously. It became clear to the old guard of the party that the new economics and new openness were corrupting the revolutionary spirit. So maybe it wasn't such a good idea to get rich first.

Bo's speech was curiously clear in meaning, for Chinese rhetoric. He was saying someone has to prosper before everyone can prosper. I think he was being so explicit because being first at anything, especially wealth, was so dangerous only a few years ago, during the Cultural Revolution. Then people were relieved of property, dignity, and often their lives for the crime of being more prosperous than their neighbors.

Much of that madness was justified by what I came to call the "ethic of mediocrity," that the decidedly second-rate was more virtuous than the excellent. In order to ensure equality, everything and everyone had to be reduced to the level of peasantry. Then, in theory, all would rise in unison to new levels. Only in this manner could both Communist purity and material gain be achieved. The sad truth is that "noble peasantry" is as much a cultural illusion for Communist theoreticians as was "noble savagery" for the Enlightenment philosophers.

When peasant standards become the cultural norm, mediocrity is both the reality and the ideal. This is the glaring weakness in Maoist Communism. It creates a mediocrity of architecture, art, science, industry, schools, and leadership.

Those who would put the lie to the "ethic of mediocrity" are antisocial and antirevolutionary. Those who can excel do so at their own risk. Some of the very able compromise their own skills, settling for shoddy standards and performance. Others become almost autistically secretive, internalizing their energy into private worlds of poetry, calligraphy, and art with hermetically private meaning. Yet others find the outlet for superior craft and wit in the "black": the widespread and growing black market economy of China.

True "China lovers," both native and foreign, experience periodic lapses in their devotion, sieges of depression during which they cannot ignore the deadening impact of class leveling. It periodically overwhelms even those who are committing their lives to the "new China." They despair even as they labor.

Hospitality

The concepts of guest, host, and hospitality are very powerful parts of the image and self-image of China. Living in China, one is continuously reminded of the guest/host relationship. Being a good guest means ignoring any negative or potentially embarrassing condition or event, while being appreciative of whatever is called to your attention. Some days there is a great deal to ignore, but you learn to follow the lead of your host.

Your everyday contacts will be marked by lateness, delays, abruptness, inexplicable schedule changes, deceit, evasiveness, preposterous gossip, and myriad other situations that seem inhospitable by Western standards. However, from the Chinese point of view, you are not supposed to acknowledge any of this, and so long as you appear to not notice you are a good guest. It would be terribly rude to call attention to these situations, because if you were meant to notice, your host would point it out to you.

The same is true of street scuffles, public arguments, beggars, rats, and the normal appearances of malnutrition and filth that you must pass on the way to a museum or a ceremony. Your host will direct your attention to what should be seen and, by example, teach you to blithely ignore the rest. We do the same thing as we ignore street people and bag ladies while directing tourists to our museums. To some degree, this is true in all cultures, but by necessity it is a major part of the guest/host relationship in China.

At the risk of sounding like an ungrateful wretch and/or "ugly American," I am trying to point out the differing interpretations placed on hospitality in the two cultures. In the U.S., hospitality consists of a series of small courtesies made to accommodate the guest. U.S. hospitality is based in preparation—some advance planning centering on the guest's daily comfort, the guest's preferences and interests, and trying to adjust to the guest's likes and dislikes.

In China, travel and communication are so iffy that preparation often leads to disappointment. Normal comfort is too scarce to be customized to the individual. Adjusting to the individual is not only antisocialist, it is anti-Confucian.

So, whereas American hospitality is most often a series of accommodations to the guest, in China it is most often an inflexible, overwhelming, food-centered display designed to embarrass the guest into acquiescence. Only a total ingrate could complain about daily life after your host has spent a month's salary or budget on one night of culinary excess. If there is not ample food left on the table after you have been virtually force-fed into semicoma, the banquet is a failure. The point is to have too much, far too much, food for any guest to consume; then Chinese hospitality has been demonstrated. All the embarrassments and inconveniences are buried by mounds of food.

The next day you still won't get a response to your request for a second chair for your living quarters, but only a boor would complain. So by Chinese rules, the Chinese always come off as more gracious than their barbarian guests. Even if it wreaks havoc with the plans or desires of the guest, the host has demonstrated hospitality with an isolated grand gesture.

The Emperor's Household

If nothing else (of course, there is much else), this sojourn reaffirmed my unwavering belief in the power of culture. Enduring, persisting, unerodible culture is all that China has had for centuries (aside from war, famine, and pestilence). The culture reemerges every day as the authorities relax their control over the many aspects of daily life that have for twenty years been contained to near-implosion. Folk medicine, folk religion, folk dress, folk wisdom, and folk foolishness all pop through the membrane of state planning. Cases in point:

A. The village behind the campus, more by collective unconsciousness than calculated decision, rebuilt a small Taoist shrine that had been pulled down during the Cultural Revolution. No one agitated for it or promised great things at its reconstruction or deplored its destruction. They simply rebuilt it as soon as it was safe to do so, because it, like the trees that shaded it, was supposed to be there. It had always been there, and now it's there again. Now it can be ignored because it's back where it's supposed to be, where it always was.

B. A grandmother bicycles, in front of me, with her grandson in the basket seat. He wears a mandarin costume, complete with skullcap and a long human-hair pigtail attached to the cap. Traditionally, this little practice of contagious magic was done to maximize the possibility that the little knee-grabber would grow up to attain a position of employment in the Imperial government—whether by self-fulfilling prophecy or mana power or bribery. Now it resurfaces, either: (1) just for the hell of it, because it looks cute and grandmothers will be grandmothers, or (2) to maximize the possibility he will grow up to be a government employee.

C. Even in the socialist state, being a government employee confers social distinctions that might be likened to being an employee of the emperor. It is top status in the classless society and "iron rice bowl" employment (though the October 1, 1986, Employment Practices Law may make the rice bowl more biodegradable for new government employees). Despite sometimes significantly higher income, a private enterpriser does not have the status of a bureaucrat, even if that bureaucrat is void of all enterprise. All those patriotic songs sung by grade school munchkins do have consequences.

Consider the situation of a local noodle-shop entrepreneur: a handsome woman in her fifties, she started a cold-drink sidewalk stand on campus as soon as free markets were sanctioned. By undercutting the university price, she cornered the market, parlayed this into one campus noodle shop, and now owns two or three more in town (though the term "noodle shop" greatly dignifies these makeshift shelters of rough timber and reed mats).

I can attest to the healthful, restorative powers of her steamed dumplings (twenty to the plate for about forty cents) and her snake soup. In the U.S., she would have been incorporated and on the verge of selling franchises. But here, she carefully donated money to finance public building in her community and concealed any sign of wealth for fear of incurring the ready envy and wrath of those on the alert for such bourgeois behavior. She worked literally twenty hours day and enjoyed only the mental freedom of knowing where her money was buried (another ancient but vital cultural practice) and the emotional pleasure of being very good at what she did.

But even liberated captainesses of industry have unrealized fantasies. Hers is that she wants her daughters to marry above their peasant origins. (Does this all begin to sound familiar to students of history and/or soap operas?) It is an open secret that she has a standing offer of many yuan to the college graduates who claim the hands of her daughters. Despite the ample allures of the daughters, the dumplings, the snake soup, the noodle empire, and the yuan, there are no takers among the college swains. This is because the pasta tyro and her offspring are low-status, self-employed achievers, while all the college grads plan to be government employees with a status similar to retainers in the emperor's household. This is the strength of culture.

Theocracy

Every ideologically dedicated community, large or small, breeds a puritanism by which the leadership can judge as acceptable or unacceptable the various aspects of modernity. In China, as among the old order Amish in northern Indiana, there clearly was a moral judgment made by the party leadership that condoned those worldly traits that promoted productiveness, and condemned those traits that precipitated self-indulgence or pleasure. For both the Amish community and the Chinese Communist party, each technological decision is also a moral decision. Both leaderships are painfully aware of the seductiveness of technological change, aware that there are always social and moral consequences to including new technology in a culture. We mainstream Westerners are either less cognizant of this or just too decadent to care. Both the Amish and the Chinese would probably say it's the latter.

Thoughts like this led me to begin thinking of China as the world's largest Anabaptist community (the Anabaptists were a radical sixteenth-century Puritan sect who lived communally). I noted the following similarities between China and the Anabaptist Christian sects:

1. Uniformity of dress and outward appearance.
2. Orthodoxy of thought based in a sacralized text—New Testament or Marxist-Leninist-Maoist thought.
3. Litany of martyrs and prophets.
4. Xenophobia—self-concept of being the pure community surrounded by decadent outsiders.
5. Suspicion of change and technology—technology for productivity is good; technology for human enrichment/leisure is bad.
6. Work ethic: work = virtue.

7. Communal ideal superior to individualism.
8. Family as the core of social existence.
9. Education limited and focused upon productive skills and social/political conservatism (outside values censored).
10. Future utopian perfection—prophesied in holy texts as Christian paradise or as workers' socialist utopia.
11. Self-image as model for the rest of mankind.
12. Puritanical value system—antiworldliness, antisexuality, anti-consumer goods, anti-private wealth.

This love-hate attitude regarding change is symptomatic of a deeper philosophical conflict that prevents China from adhering to the direct path of modernity. In the classroom, when teaching the issues of cultural change, I try to convey the difference between a pure theocracy and a pure technocracy.

By "theocracy," I mean a society in which the institution of moral-social leadership (usually a church or religion, but in the twentieth century also an ideology) is the dominant institutional force by which all successful change must be approved. A "technocracy" is a society in which technical-economic development is the most powerful institutional force, and all moral-social judgments are compromised, mitigated, and rationalized to condone what is technically feasible. There are no pure forms of either, but the United States is well along the path of becoming a technocracy; while China, like Albania and some Moslem states, remains essentially a theocracy.

Nearly all nations, of course, want it both ways; they want moral-social continuity and technical-economic growth. The image of the U.S. that I use to belabor my point in the classroom is that the U.S. wants the Walton family in outer space: we want nineteenth-century agrarian values, the traditional extended family, and the virtues of home and hearth illuminated by laser technology.

This all becomes relevant in the history of nations at those times when they just can't have it both ways. What does a nation do when it is forced to choose between moral-social continuity and technical-economic change? Forced to choose, a modern society (technocracy) will opt for technical-economic growth at the expense of moral-social continuity. Forced to choose; a traditional society (theocracy) will value moral-social continuity at the cost of technical-economic growth. No country wishes to sacrifice one for the other, yet at critical historical moments, all must do so. This is the cutting edge that separates modern nation-states from traditional cultures.

For better or worse, the U.S. has obviously made the choice for modernity. In China, the choices take on dramatic proportion because the weight of the past and the needs of the present are both so great. Thus, China sways traumatically through waves of modernization and ebbs of backlash with the outcome still uncertain.

China or "Not"

Much has been made by scholars such as Lynn White, Jr., of the oneness or sense of commonality that pervades Eastern thinking. This usually is preliminary to pointing out that dualistic thinking results in the Western view of humans being separate from one another, from other creatures, and from the environment, and how this leads to terrible social relations and environmental pillage. Of course there is a grain of truth here, but that grain could never constitute the entire loaf of planetary guilt that White, Alan Watts, and other sixties philosophers tried to impose on Western dualistic thinking.

Historically in China, the absence of differentiation or duality has been reinforced by Confucianism, Buddhism, and by the Maoist version of Marxism. Confucian thought throughout its centuries of influence always held to the dictum of loyalty to the family unit and filial piety as prerequisites of a virtuous life. A person has no real identity outside of family and the expression of obedience and devotion to the family patriarch. That is the very essence of Confucian virtue. The correct relationship between person and nation is the organic extension of this principle. Obedience, devotion, and piety are due the ultimate family unit—China. Every government that has ruled China for the last 2,000 years saw the wisdom of encouraging this perception. One reason China can say it absorbs every conqueror is that every new leader attempts to wrap his reign in the cloak of Confucianism.

When Buddhism entered China, there was no conflict between the dictates of filial piety and the Four Great Truths. The Buddhist teachings against "separate selfhood" and "ego-desire" and the Confucian attitudes of obedience to authority were mutually supportive.

Attaching Communism to Confucianism was a very natural grafting of one group-centered philosophy on another. Now, with the "open policy" of Chairman Deng, there is every likelihood that Chinese Communism will become increasingly Chinese and decreasingly Marxist-Leninist. Maybe a better label for China in the twenty-first century would be "Communist Confucianism"!

Yet, even though Chinese are free to practice religion, the ceremonial and ritual core of Buddhist life is critically labeled as "feudalism." It is primarily among the minorities in frontier provinces that Buddhism openly exists. The Buddhist reverence for life expressed in the Eightfold Noble Path as "right livelihood" is severely undermined and has no practical application regarding what Lynn White, Jr., called "the environmental ethic." This reverence is reserved for Socialist Reality, not planetary ecology.

Similarly, the elements of Confucianism that remain condemned as feudal are the ceremonial aspects perceived as supportive of traditional class and status distinctions. What remains is a raw Confucianism stripped of ritual, with the dictums of obedience and loyalty to authority its monotone message.

The result has been that a kind of beehive intelligence and behavior has been encouraged by the worst tendencies in the communal ethic and reinforced by the reign of terror called the Cultural Revolution. To this day in the countryside and even in the lesser urban centers the cautious survivors conceal any cultured or sophisticated tendencies that might be labeled "bourgeois-liberal."

Homes retain a studied drabness that will not distinguish them from the residences of other workers. Most bicycles follow Henry Ford's dictum, "Any color you want, so long as it's black." Though the Mao suit is less ubiquitous, it remains the safest cloak of invisibility. Of course, material scarcity is one reason for this uniformity, but those who prefer more and can afford it still fear the consequences of flaunting different tastes or standards. Privately, the most sophisticated will voice their need to not appear non-Chinese.

To my original point: what I perceive now in China is a beehive mentality that perceives the world as what is Chinese (in all its nuances) and what is not. The "not" is anything that cannot be comprehended as a nuance of China or be absorbed as part of the "new" China. "The West" really means "not China." The only parts of the West that interest China are parts that can be brought into the hive to be ingested by China and become Chinese. The rest of the West is simply "not"—it has no meaning. The Chinese interpreter assigned to me at the university was avid about learning aspects of American life that might be useful to teaching English in China or that might advance his desire to study in the U.S. However, when a conversation among him and two Westerners moved to other Western ideas, he dozed off.

We Westerners think binominally, in terms of a thing and its opposite. Therefore we can become interested in objects, acts, and ideas different from our own; and we can retain interest in an absolute opposite (things utterly different from our own experience). We can study and even empathize with an act, idea, or object dichotomously—without having to make it a nuance or extension of ourselves.

The Chinese think monomially of acts, ideas, and objects as only China and nuances of China. They are never really interested in another way unless it can become the Chinese way. They truly have no interest in Western culture unless it can be incorporated into Chinese culture. If it cannot be absorbed into China, then it becomes part of the "not."

But once a thing is made a nuance or part of China, then it is Chinese—regardless of the facts. For example, socialism is now considered Chinese and in no way Western. The wave of rhetoric against "bourgeois liberalism" is utter nonsense until one realizes this. The government news organs, such as *Renmim Ribao* (*People's Daily*) and the *Beijing Review,* continuously attacked Western ideas as antisocialist during 1987. The January 19, 1987, *Beijing Review* even republished a *Renmin Ribao* commentary entitled, "Complete Westernization Negates Socialism." This illustrates my point: there is now no official or public recognition in China that Marxist socialism is itself a Western idea absorbed by modern China. Continually in the Chinese press and in scholarship you can read of Marxism as something outside of Western thought, with no acknowledgment that Marx and Lenin are major elements of the fabric of Western thought. It is as though socialism and Marxist-Leninism have no history prior to their Chinese liberation. Now that China has claimed them, they are *not* Western, and their history before being ingested into China is a part of the *not.*

To repeat my point, the Chinese do not think about or hold interest in something that is not China; they think only in terms of China and what can be an extension of China. This is the very real sense in which their thinking differs from ours.

Relative Freedoms

Erich Fromm once wrote that the psychological dimension of freedom is loneliness; that the pure state of freedom means being utterly alone to act and think without being inhibited by concern for others. And he observed that the majority of human beings will always sacrifice freedom for group acceptance. For a Chinese, being alone is like being buried alive. Their entire life is spent in constant and contiguous contact with family and the communal extension of family. An unattended child is simply not seen in China. A sibling or grandparent or surrogate is available whenever the parents must be absent. The Chinese are most cheerful under conditions Americans consider crowded.

Perhaps this is why there has never been any possibility that freedom, as Americans understand it, could or would become a reality there. The escape from freedom Fromm describes as the basis of the mass acceptance of totalitarianism will always be preferred over solitary decision making and personal responsibility by those who have internalized Chinese Confucianist culture.

Since there is no period in the long history of China when freedom (as Americans or Fromm think of it) existed, most Chinese cannot notice its absence. In fact, most Chinese consider themselves free; they truly feel they have freedom, even though they cannot change jobs or residences, or even travel outside their province without government permission. Their futures are wholly dependent upon the favor of the unit superiors who hold their identity papers. Yet in their minds—minds not exposed to books, film, television, newspapers, or art that does not correspond to the state's interests, they are free—free to function as contented extensions of their group. That is the essence of Chinese freedom.

At the other end of the political spectrum, we consider ourselves free—truly free, even while we are pressured by our culture's values to continuously change jobs and residences, and to leave behind family and friends in an endless pursuit of wealth and status. Our futures are dependent on our skill and good luck in negotiating these material pursuits, while we are distracted by a barrage of information from the entertainment media whose disparate messages hardly correspond with anyone's interests. We are free to negotiate this maelstrom on our own, sinking or surviving. That is the essence of American individualism.

What the most conservative elements of the party leadership in China fear most from students returning from studying abroad is that they may be infected with this foreign sense of freedom. From either a Confucianist or Communist viewpoint, it is unhealthy.

The Myth of Modernization

Back in the pre-Marxist history of European socialism (which the Chinese Marxists virtually ignore), George Sorel was writing about the "myth of the general strike." He meant "myth" in the creative sense that a universally shared belief could be consequential in shaping events to match the group's ideological fantasy. In other words, the general strike might never be a reality, but the belief in it could alter the existing reality.

The longer I observed China's socialist state, the more it seemed Sorelian rather than Marxist. The important myth here is "modernization." Every day the government and its newspapers, television, and the rest of the controlled news media hammer away at perpetuating the myth of modernization. Enclaves of modern industry and technology, of course, exist; but they seem like microdots in a football field when you perceive the huge areas between them, where life remains unchanged by the twentieth century. But there you are to focus on Socialist Realism, not reality. By the inexorable laws of Socialist Realism, the existence of one microdot of modernization proves conclusively that the entire country will soon be a macrofield of modernity as long as all Chinese fervently share the myth. And, much like Reformation theology, doubt itself is a sin.

That is why there comes a time when a foreigner must either become a believer in China or leave. In most cultures, as you learn how the culture works, things get easier. In China, as you learn how it works things get harder because it is so difficult to ignore the half-truths, duplicities, evasions, and illusions of the myth of modernization. You become either a believer in Socialist Realism or a social heretic to be cast out.

SEVEN

✧ ✧ ✧ ✧ ✧ ✧

Leaving

Going Home

In the month or two before the end of any foreign living assignment, you reach the stage where it is hard simultaneously to invest energy in new experiences while you are preparing to leave. It's at this stage that we foreigners begin to tell one another that soon we're going home to distant, disparate corners of the earth. It's a curious time in which friends get together and pleasurably exchange plans to permanently part.

It was at this stage that Mary and I decided to organize a banquet for the Aussies (who had hosted us several times at their forestry compound outside Nanning) and the other foreigners—a grand total of twenty-three.

The next time you are bored, try negotiating a banquet with a Chinese chef. The disarmament talks are a pale imitation of hard bargaining. I can take no credit; Mary sensibly decided that

I had not yet attained the spirituality required for this mythic struggle of wills. She and Qing Mai handled the whole thing. Then she spent literally one whole day getting a phone call through to the Aussies. She started trying in the morning, and the call was completed at 6:40 P.M. (There's no use trying to explain this to someone who hasn't lived in similar circumstances.)

My part in this psychodrama was to play Paul Revere, bicycling to various campuses and confirming time and date—good training for the Grand Prix. Then I bought wine and a carton of Marlboros for the cook. These were the lynchpin of the final agreement. We did have the proviso that the wine was handed over only after the food was cooked.

The banquet, like most of the social occasions at that time, was an enjoyable but bittersweet affair, as I was aware throughout the toasting and joking that the room was filled with nice people I would never see again and with whom my life had become surprisingly involved.

Amusing the Stone

To repair the sky, 36,501 blocks of stone were cut. Only 36,500 were used. The solitary rejected stone lay in a deep depression (pun intended) until noticed by the Buddhist Monk of Infinite Space and the Taoist Priest of Boundless Time. For the stone's edification, they transported it to the world of humans, where it witnessed and has inscribed upon itself the joys, sorrows, and foolishness of generations of mortals.

After such generations, perhaps eons, of people watching, the stone was noticed by a Taoist called Reverend Void (what a great name for a TV evangelist) who read on the stone's engraved facades of the stone's rejection, its transportation to the realm of humans, and its observation of endless human activity. Finding it all no better or worse than any other account of human history, he copied it and took it away to be published. Thus it passed into human hands—a cavalcade of generations of human folly unwittingly played out to entertain, educate, and cheer up a rock.

This is the purported origin of *A Dream of Red Mansions*, and I can think of no reason to doubt the veracity of this pedigree. *A Dream of Red Mansions* is a classic of Chinese literature. Mary was deep in its volumes at the same time it was produced on Chinese television, so we tried to follow the text as we watched its dramatization. The murkiness of my own language comprehension added to the mythically surreal wooziness of its space and time.

This was at the same time when I had been reflecting on my own journey—the miles traveled; the conditions endured; the thrills, boredom, tiny achievements, and chronic frustrations of being a foreigner; the lingering numbness in my face—and had been reckless enough to ask myself why? Now I had an answer: because it's written on the stone. At that time, this answer satisfied me more than any other. There seemed no more sensible reason for having gone to China or for now going home. It was all just to entertain the stone.

Remembering There

Now when I read of China, "the modernizing world power," the China of newspaper headlines and magazine covers, I wonder if I was really there. That China is less familiar to me now than before my ten months in the place of the same name. I wonder, when reading or hearing other people's descriptions, if we went to the same country. Of course we didn't, in any experiential sense. China is too vast in size, too layered in time to take in whole, so we each can only report the pieces we experienced.

So when I think of China, it is of minuscule pieces where, if returned by luck or magic, I could find my way by bicycle or foot through mazes of streets, footpaths, and alleyways. I think of the feeling of being absorbed into a stream of people and bicycles, and of the smells and sounds. Though buildings are being razed daily in Nanning, I could find my way to wet markets, street restaurants, and shops. I could recognize the sound of brooms scratching on pavement in the early morning outside my window; the screech of a particular dining-hall tricycle with a bent wheel rubbing its frame, carrying breakfast supplies from the university kitchens; the sound of the padding feet of the old woman in the apartment above our own, as she took her health walk back and forth across her room. I would be able to identify the worst cigarette smokers in our building by their morning coughing fits. I could recognize the feel and dusty smell of the mosquito netting near my pillow. It is tiny insignificant details and normal people that comprise the China I now remember.

I am still amazed that, at a point on a map thousands of miles from where I now call home, I know the noodle lady, the blind palmist, teachers, party secretaries, black marketeers, bicycle repairmen, and so many young men and women who were my students—all making their own journeys of accommodation to the life that is possible for them.

When I think of China, I think of people left behind who were decent and caring. I receive their letters, return greetings, send tiny gifts, and know that I am a thin, fragile lifeline, which in their fantasies might carry them to another life. Yet most of them know they are ill suited and unprepared for any other world.

For them, I am like a rare, exotic, small-brained bird of outrageous plumage that fell to earth in their garden, whooped and thrashed about, amazed and entertained them, then again, gracelessly, became airborne and swooped away. For me, they remain my captor-stewards, who sustained me when I was too dumb to feed and shelter myself, then waved and waved as I abandoned the restricting caged shelter they had provided. They are the friends I will not see again. Each of us has receded in the distance to tiny forms; but periodically we return, large in one another's memories and dreams.

Perhaps the best ending is a myth of origin: The Na-Khi of Yunnan Province compensate for the sparseness of their material life with an elaborate religious tradition that includes more than one myth of origin. The version I prefer reveals that Shadows existed first. From Shadows came Mother, Reality, Unreality, Competence, and Incompetence. These caused a magic or inter-course (the same Na-Khi phrase has both meanings) that produced a brilliant object—the First Great Cause. From further magic or intercourse between Unreality and Incompetence came the First Evil Cause—the enemy of the First Great Cause.

It doesn't seem to me that any theological or philosophical thinking of the last few thousand years, Eastern or Western, has been an improvement on this formulation.

APPENDIX

Guidebooks abound for the tourist who essentially is going to migrate between historical site, scenic wonder, and hotel. Similarly, there are several guidebooks haughtily aimed not at tourists, but at travelers who are going to trek, backpack, rough it, and/or move about on a shoestring. Almost all of them have some useful advice.

Less is written for those who intend to settle in and work or study for an extended time in China. So here are two lists I compiled for friends and inquirers who were contemplating going to China for those reasons.

*Thirty-Three Things to Do or Think about
to Make a Year in China Less Uncomfortable
(In No Particular Order)*

1. Learn as much language as possible. Even a few words are better than none. Taking classes is best, if they're available and you have time. Accept the fact that you will sound like a fool at first. Better at home among friends than in China (but you will sound like a fool there also).

    Study from cassettes as much as possible. Your classes and tapes will probably be in Mandarin. If you are going south of Shanghai or to western China, most people will not sound like the cassette, but it will all help. Cantonese is quite different and many of the southern minority dialects will be incomprehensible, but go ahead and study your Mandarin. The Chinese who *want* to understand you will figure out what you're saying. Those who don't want to understand you won't, even if you speak perfectly. Once immersed in China, you will acquire "street Chinese" that will suffice for shopping, traveling, buying tickets, and so forth.

2. Definitely have a physical exam before leaving, if for no other reason than to assure yourself that you will recover when you begin to acquire the inevitable colds, viruses, and intestinal flare-ups. The only inoculation you absolutely should have is tetanus-diphtheria. Phone the local Public Health Department to get advisories on current outbreaks of disease.

3. Bring aspirin, multivitamins, antibiotic salve, Band-Aids, paper tissues, and those little foil-packed wet towelettes. None of these are readily available outside of Beijing or Shanghai, and all of them will be very comforting at some point.

4. Dentistry is a vastly underdeveloped medical science in China. Have absolutely all possibly needed dentistry attended to before leaving home. Never consider going to a dentist in China. If you have a dental problem while in China, the only acceptable solution is to fly to Hong Kong.

5. Bring a truly minimal number of casual clothes appropriate to the weather of the area where you will be. Unless you are working for the State Department, you will not need dressy clothes and suits. Most of what you bring will be ruined during your stay, so don't bring anything you love. Bring nothing requiring ironing or dry cleaning.

 You can't find good shoes in China, so be sure yours are comfortable and durable. Casual-style walking shoes will be appropriate anywhere.

6. Months before you leave for China, begin mailing your books. Send them by surface mail. It will take two or three months, but air mail is prohibitively expensive for heavy boxes, even at book rate. Send books you will need for your

work, as well as books to inform and entertain you. Once you're there, books in your own language are like diamonds.

Be sure to make a list of all books shipped and keep the list with you. Some books (I couldn't figure out any pattern) will either be stolen or confiscated in Chinese customs. Don't waste energy complaining. Nothing can be done; everything will be denied. As your Foreign Affairs Office will be powerless to do anything about it, they will lose face if you complain. Then you will be the source of their difficulty. So just accept your losses quietly.

Many situations like this will arise during your stay. If you have a problem but there's clearly no way to correct it, calling attention to it will only result in loss of face to your Chinese hosts, and then they will become increasingly reluctant to deal with you, even in situations where they can help.

7. Re-record as much of your favorite music as possible on long-playing cassettes, so you can pack several albums onto a few cassettes. Also bring two or three blank tapes.

8. The best parting gifts for special Chinese friends, when you leave China, will be books and music.

9. Before leaving home, find out if your Chinese employer will furnish you with a cassette/short-wave radio. The BBC and Voice of America are very welcome sounds while in China. If you must, bring a small but powerful unit with you. Maybe you'll want to buy one in Hong Kong, but there aren't many bargains in electronics left in Hong Kong. For those types of items, your local discount store is probably cheaper.

10. Read as many travel guides as you can without buying one. They're expensive and heavy to carry. Photocopy relevant pages. If you do want to carry one, the Lonely Planet Publication *China: A Travel Survival Kit* is very well written and researched.

11. Read as many books on Chinese culture and history as you can absorb. But don't think they will prepare you for the

assault on your senses that is China. Everyone develops their own China bibliography that includes works by John King Fairbank, Jonathan Spence, Fox Butterfield, Sterling Seagrave, Richard Solomon, etc.

A new anthology that is banned in the P.R.C. is called *Seeds of Fire, Chinese Voices of Conscience.* It is well worth examining before you enter China.

12. If you are going to teach, photocopy multiples of short (one- or two-page), not-very-complicated articles. Mail these (by surface mail) months in advance. No matter where you teach in China, you will not have adequate English-language materials.

13. Mail (by surface mail), months in advance, the following: pencils, pens, rubber bands, paperclips, tape (all kinds), carbon paper, notepads, and large envelopes. Some of it will disappear in transit.

14. Don't forget a paperback dictionary for your own use.

15. Bring whatever cosmetic and toilet articles you think you can't live without. After you use them up, you'll live without them. Everybody who stays in China for more than a month begins to look like they've been on a six-month camping trip.

16. Bring with you the legal limit of color film (twenty-five rolls per person). Slide film is very difficult to get developed in China. The quality of developing for any color film is very inconsistent. Bring color print film, as well as slide film, as the Chinese friends you photograph will want to see the photos.

Before you leave home, take slides or photos of your everyday life—the grocery store, shopping center, post office, your car, street scenes, your kitchen, refrigerator, etc. (Remember, one person's mundane life is another's exotica.)

17. Bring a Swiss army knife and a small container of a few dozen nails and screws. Bring a small flashlight and long-life

batteries. The Chinese brand of battery is named "White Elephant"—does that tell you something?

18. If you intend to cook, bring baking powder and the seasonings you enjoy. Salt, soy, ginger, and garlic are about the only familiar seasonings you'll find in the market.

19. If your current employers are sending you to China, bug them with every possible question about your Chinese employment, work, living conditions, etc. Take nothing for granted. Be obnoxious before you leave for China, then you will have to spend less time being obnoxious when you get there.

20. Negotiate your teaching load (or work load) before you leave. Do not agree to more courses than you want to teach. As you will have almost no clerical help, your classes will take lots of time. Agree only to your normal work load or less. (Many Chinese faculty teach only four hours per week.)

21. For the above reason, believe very little that is told to you or written to you. But get everything that is important to you in writing, and then cling to it through everything that follows. Take copies of all letters and agreements with you. Point to them, even when it seems useless.

22. Living and traveling in China seem very inexpensive when you are receiving a Western salary. Once you are in the Chinese economy, being paid a Chinese salary, it does not seem so cheap.

23. Bring a money pouch or belt to wear while traveling in China. Until 1987 the ten-yuan note was the largest currency denomination. Now there are 50 Y and 100 Y denominations, but few are circulated outside of banks. So, while traveling you may carry several thousand yuan, all in 10 Y notes.

24. Start cutting U.S. postage stamps off your letters and mail. Bring them with you to give as small presents. The Chinese are avid stamp collectors.

25. Learn to use chopsticks. It's easier to practice at home than to learn at a Chinese banquet.

26. In China, buy a package of cheap chopsticks to carry with you for when you eat at street restaurants. You can avoid a lot of germs by having your own sticks. Buy the cheap ones, because you'll forget to take them with you after eating.

27. Toothpaste (very sweet-tasting), soap, and toilet paper are all available, but it's nice to not have to worry about buying them the first couple of weeks.

28. On the flight over, take tranquilizers or whatever you need to get maximum sleep. If you can sleep the entire flight, you won't miss a thing, and you will soon need the energy.

29. At the San Francisco or Los Angeles airport, if not before, change at least $10.00 U.S. into Hong Kong dollars for the airport taxi.

30. In Hong Kong, if you lay over a day or more, have business cards printed in English and Chinese. The Chinese exchange business cards at every opportunity.

31. As you receive the boxes you mailed to yourself, open them carefully and save them for mailing things home. Boxes and containers for mailing are very difficult to get in China.

32. Before leaving home, send a mailing tube to yourself in China. Stick a calendar in it, so an empty tube doesn't baffle customs. Paintings and prints are among the best things to buy in China and a mailing tube is virtually impossible to locate.

33. Be prepared to perform at Chinese parties and public occasions. It is natural for them to sing songs for one another's entertainment. It is not so natural for Westerners. So if you are not musically talented, be forewarned: you will have to sing for your supper somewhere along the way. It doesn't matter what (I always did "Home on the Range," quite off-key).

Ten Chinese Bureaucratic Rules of the Game
When Dealing with Foreigners

1. No decision always is better than any decision, including the right decision. This is the first rule of survival at all levels of Chinese bureaucracy. The perfect administrator is one who does nothing and obstructs everything. The perfect assistant is one who prevents all communication to his superior and recognizes no one inferior to himself. All decisions are ultimately dangerous. Even decisions correct at the time and credited to you can ultimately be viewed as incorrect and held against you. Do nothing and retire to a peaceful old age; do anything and forever fear its consequences.

2. If you are forced to make a decision, put it off as long as possible. Use any and every excuse. Later is always better than now.

3. When non-Chinese want something, Chinese always stress the need for patience. When Chinese want something of non-Chinese, they always stress that the Chinese have been patient, but now the situation is urgent, even desperate.

4. In China, an agreement is sacred when you agree. A little later, it is just one more thing that needs to be reconsidered. What Westerners consider reneging or even welching is just good business if it's the Chinese doing it. It is dishonorable if it's a non-Chinese doing it.

5. Saying that you are going to do something is equivalent to planning for it. Or at least it is all the planning you will do in advance of the event.

6. One can never give too many speeches, or the same speech too many times, or mouth too many clichés.

7. Never tell a foreigner anything in advance. It is better that they are always unprepared and slightly off-balance.

8. In negotiation, see to it that foreigners negotiate at all levels of the bureaucracy—local, provincial, and national. That way, in the interest of harmony, they will concede a little at each level; and overall, they will concede a lot.

9. In negotiation, when foreigners are on a tight travel schedule, see to it that the business meetings are placed at the end of the schedule. Fill the preceding time with tours, banquets, and entertainment so that the foreigner is groggy, tired, MSG-loaded, and anxious to complete any deal (not the best deal) in the inadequate time left for negotiating—so his trip won't be a total loss. Foreigners like to complete things. Chinese know nothing is ever completed.

10. It is better to lie than face any unpleasant truth. This is called "Socialist Realism."